Boomerrrang...

To Marica

Best on This Journey

Boomerrrang...

The Amazing Journey of Two New England Boomers...How They
Chose Their Dream Retirement Home...and Why They Left...

*She and her long-time partner searched for their perfect retirement
home up and down the East coast, for almost ten years, and then they
came to Asheville, often called "one of the best retirement towns in the
United States."*
Here's what happened......

COLLEEN KELLY MELLOR

ISBN: 1978367309
ISBN 13: 9781978367302

Foreword

The 19th century Impressionist painters, Degas, Monet, and Renoir created works of art that emphasized the artist's perception of the subject matter, as much as the subject itself.

In borrowing their style, *Boomerrrang* seeks to convey my writer's perception of one of America's most popular retirement towns, Asheville, via short colorful pieces, woven together as a tapestry, akin to the colorful quilts created by artisans in the region.

Perhaps it is no surprise that to appreciate the region fully, I needed to step back and view it from afar, after having lived in its midst for almost nine years. I wrote this book during the two years after we left.

I found that, like impressionistic paintings, Asheville's colorful scenes were best appreciated when regarded from afar.

My accounts are my perception seen through the lens of my personal, as well as my professional life, as realtor. My knowledge acquired through my career helped us avoid costly mistakes as home buyers new to a region. I now share this treasure trove of tips with readers.

Others who bought, uninformed, weren't nearly so fortunate.

Finally, my book opens with the medical crisis we endured as a result of a freak accident on a mountain road behind our townhome complex. What made it especially unnerving? We'd left the frenetic pace of the Northeast for a simpler, slower pace of life in western North Carolina. With this accident and its fall-out, we were kicked into a never-ending nightmare of Homeric proportions.

Perhaps those put all else in perspective.

Table of Contents

Foreword · v

Part I: Death and Rebirth · 1
The Crash: April 10, 2010 · 3
Paul "Dies" · 7
Quagmire · 10
He's "Bonkers" and I'm Terrified · · · · · · · · · · · · · · · · · · 14
At War · 17
Long Road to Recovery · 21
Our "Out-of-Towners'" Airline Disaster Story · · · · · · · · · · · 24
An Angel Appears · 28
Regrouping and Final Decision-Making · · · · · · · · · · · · · · 30
Hope Out of Ashes: *Grandpa and the Truck* Books · · · · · · · · 37
Dry Run at Sale · 43
We Sell · 48
What We Did with the Furniture · · · · · · · · · · · · · · · · · · 58
Legal Mayhem · 62
Why We Left Asheville · 67
One Year Out from Sale · 71

Part II: We Adjust to Our New Region · · · · · · · · · · · · · 77
How We Chose Our Retirement State · · · · · · · · · · · · · · · 79
First Overtures · 85

Was Our Choice of Asheville Subliminal? · · · · · · · · · · · · · · 91
Who We Are · 95
Why We're Not Naples, Florida Folks · · · · · · · · · · · · · · 99
Love at First Sight (OK, Maybe Not "First") · · · · · · · · · · · ·102
Townhome/Condo Living · 106
Friend-Making in a New Land · · · · · · · · · · · · · · · · · · ·112
Friend-Losing in a New Land: "Rest in Peace, Ralph…" · · · · · ·116
Franklin's Caffe Rel, Friends' Mountain Retreat,
and Treasure-Hunting · 120
Thrash About?...Keep Still?... · · · · · · · · · · · · · · · · · · · 123
Quick Take on Towns Outside Asheville · · · · · · · · · · · · · · 126
The Precipitous Learning Curve of "Reverse Halfbacks" · · · · ·131
Bliss for a While...Then Another Kind of Crash · · · · · · · · · · 134
Even in Asheville, the Spiritual Goes Awry · · · · · · · · · · · · 138
I Go to Jail ·144
I'm an Avatar ·147
The Bells of Beaver Lake, North Asheville · · · · · · · · · · · · 150
Asheville and Surrounds: Land of Contradictions · · · · · · · · ·153

Part III: What You Might *Not Like* About the Region · · · · · · ·157
Weekends Are Different There · · · · · · · · · · · · · · · · · · · 159
Snow Is Serious in the South ·162
Doctors Not Easily Accessible for Two-State Folks · · · · · · · · 166
Asheville Woman Looking for a Man? "Good Luck!" · · · · · · · ·172
Bad Boys in Trucks ·175
Kudzu ·178

Part IV: What You'll *Like* About the Region · · · · · · · · · · · ·181
Craigslist Respondents Are Colorful There · · · · · · · · · · · · ·183
Asheville Crafts Are Real Art ·187
Carl Sandburg's "Connemara" ·191
Roadways Are Superb (for the most part) · · · · · · · · · · · · · 194

Top Marketer Shows the Value of His "Other Craft" · · · · · · · ·197
You Can Wear Whatever You Want · · · · · · · · · · · · · · · · · 202
Silver Is "the New Black" · 205
Two Can Eat Out as Cheaply as One (in New England) · · · · 209
It's a Dog's World ...Unless You've Got a Cat · · · · · · · · · · · ·212
True Grits and Southern Gentility · · · · · · · · · · · · · · · · · ·215
In Asheville, Police Respond (Too) Quickly · · · · · · · · · · · ·219
Yoga and Yogis Are Everywhere · · · · · · · · · · · · · · · · · · 222
Continuing Yoga...The Fart Heard
'Round the (Yoga) World· 226
You Can Celebrate Friends "Downton Abbey" Style · · · · · · · 229
Three S's and WSJ... for $50.00 a Month · · · · · · · · · · · · · · 232
Food Shopping Fun...But Could Be Better · · · · · · · · · · · · 235
Heart-Stopping Medical Folk · 238
North Carolina Back Roads: Norman Rockwell's America· · · ·241

**Bonus Booklet: Realtor's Mini-Guide for Buying/Selling
Property...Anywhere**· 245
Buying and Selling Property ·247
How Realtors Get Paid (and Why You Need to
Understand This) · 249
Is Your Realtor Really "Your Realtor"? · · · · · · · · · · · · · · 253
State You Claim as "Primary Residence" Matters · · · · · · · · 256
That Annoying "Two-State Shuffle" · · · · · · · · · · · · · · · · 259
Rent Storage Units? Not This Boomer · · · · · · · · · · · · · · 262
Hidden Monsters--Superfund Sites· · · · · · · · · · · · · · · · 265
Successful Home Buyer's Checklist· · · · · · · · · · · · · · · · · 272
Successful Home Seller's Checklist· · · · · · · · · · · · · · · · · 276

Acknowledgments· 281
The Takeaway· 283

"Be careful for what you ask."(You might get it.) All Paul and I thought we wanted was a retirement home in a warmer, less frenzied region than the Northeast. We got it . . .
. . . THAT was the problem.

Part I: Death and Rebirth

The Crash: April 10, 2010

Four of us women sat in a booth at the Stoney Knob Restaurant, in Weaverville, North Carolina, laughing hysterically, as we shared stories about our lives and the crazy situations we'd encountered. The brunch was our last get-together before Paul and I headed back to Rhode Island.

Or so I thought.

In the midst of the jocularity, my cell phone rang. I looked at the ID and saw it was Paul, so, just like that television cell carrier commercial where the young man tries, unsuccessfully, to call his girlfriend, when he's being sucked up by an alien spacecraft, I neglected to answer it, saying "Oh, it's just Paul...I'll see him in a half hour anyway."

Minutes later, my phone rang again, and I knew something was very wrong, indeed. When I answered it, a policeman said: "Mrs. Gates, there's been an accident. I'm with your husband and they're taking him to the hospital in an ambulance. Can you come?"

I told him I'd be right there, ended the call, and sat stunned.

My friends, realizing I was in shock, drove me to the hospital. Along the way, I tried desperately to quell my fear that saw me blipped back in time to a far uglier period of my life when I fought for my own survival against a medical industry that had little regard for my reality. I hoped things would be different this time.

3

Paul was taken to a state-of-the-art hospital in the region, where on any given day, thousands of patients cross its thresholds to access the services touted on its website and the billboards that greet travelers along the main thoroughfares of I-26 and I-40. Its reputation is one of the many reasons we settled in Asheville as our retirement town.

I was taken to an examination room in the emergency wing where I found Paul in significant pain, saying repeatedly that his arm was "on fire." Medics had put him in a hard neck collar to minimize movement, and he lay atop a flat board. Since I'd never heard him complain of pain in the seventeen years I'd known him, I knew his discomfort was severe.

"Is it possible to get this man something for pain?" I eventually asked a nurse. At my prompting, they gave him a shot of morphine and he quieted down.

Over the next several hours, Paul lay on that board as hospital staff determined what to do. "Will he be brought to a room soon?" I asked the young, attending neurosurgeon. "Oh, no," he responded, "He's most likely going home today. He'll probably wear a collar for a few weeks." He never looked at me directly, when he spoke, but continued to jot down notes regarding Paul, on his paperwork.

I was amazed to hear him suggest Paul's injuries were minor. To me, Paul's pain was extraordinary, and I wondered how we'd cope at home when the effects of the morphine wore off.

Over the next several hours, we discovered that this doctor's initial assessment was wrong. Paul wouldn't be going home, after all. His neck was broken between the fourth and sixth vertebrae. He'd need surgery, as soon as possible.

In the meantime, he'd be kept immobilized in that collar and medicated, so as to limit movement.

In that examination room later on, we had a visitor who'd asked to see Paul. She was the driver who caused all the mayhem, a pretty little twelve-year-old girl who'd begged her uncle to let her "practice drive" that day. More surprising still, he allowed it. He'd apparently sat beside her in his GMC truck. She'd slammed into Paul's car as he rounded the curve on that narrow mountain road.

Paul had gone to the top of that mountain road behind our complex for one last look over the town of Weaverville, before we headed back to Rhode Island. On past occasions, we'd both driven up for the view; we'd even contemplated building a home there, some day.

From the police report, we learned that the girl was coming down that mountain road and panicked when she couldn't get the brakes to work. Then too, she wore flip-flops. (I saw the bejeweled pair on her when she came to visit him.)

I have my own theory: At barely five feet tall, she doubtless couldn't even reach the brakes, and when the truck picked up speed and hurtled down that mountain road, she steered it in towards the mountain side, crossing over into Paul's lane.

When he rounded the curve, she hit him head-on. He never saw her coming—until it was too late.

Following impact, Paul heard her crying, asking the policeman: "Is that man all right?"

Ironically, both the girl and he were shuttled to the hospital in the same ambulance, but the girl had minor injuries and was released. However, she asked the medical staff if she could come and apologize to Paul.

I told them that I thought her apologizing would be a good thing, but I wanted no one from her family, coming in with her.

When she saw him, she fell apart, sobbing, telling him how sorry she was. I got up from my chair and hugged her, for I didn't blame her for what happened. She was a child. The responsibility for the accident lay with the supposed "uncle" who'd allowed her behind the wheel.

Below is what's left of Paul's Sebring that he took for a short spin up that mountain road, behind our townhome complex, on that fateful day that would signal so much more trouble for us.

Paul "Dies"

Paul's surgery was a complicated ordeal lasting nine hours—more than twice as long as the neurosurgeon anticipated.

We, in his family, hung out in a visitor waiting room for news of the outcome. The doctor gave me his surgical report, as we stood in a crowded, noisy corridor. I struggled to take in the details.

The fourth and fifth cervical discs in Paul's neck required fusion where the fraction occurred, and the doctor had strengthened the adjoining area that had been compromised. He revealed a chilling detail: If a bone touching Paul's spinal cord had gone another inch, it might have severed his spinal cord. Paul was lucky. He might have been completely paralyzed.

I left the hospital in the wee hours of the morning, after Paul had regained consciousness. Following hours in the recovery room, he was assigned to a step-down room where he'd presumably spend the next several days. I was surprised that he hadn't been assigned to Intensive Care, considering the doctor's statement that the surgery was "long and difficult."

The next day we, in the family, hovered over him. Paul's daughter, Amy, her husband, Jerry, and son, Sebastian, had made the trip from Rhode Island; Paul's brother, David, flew in from Arkansas.

We were all there in that room to lend our support. We laughed, cracked jokes, and generally whiled away the time. Paul was understandably sore and woozy, but he was alert and in good spirits.

Shortly after the 4:00 P.M. shift change, two nurses came in. One checked Paul's vital signs, while the other looked at his chart. My attention was aroused when the one who'd directed Paul to stick out his tongue called out for the other nurse to come and have a look.

"What's the problem?" I asked, with obvious concern. "His tongue's swollen," the nurse said. Her colleague looked at it, said nothing, and went back to what she'd been doing.

Believing him in good hands, I left the hospital at about 9:00 P.M.. Three long days of tension and anxiety had sapped my last bit of energy. The rest of the family had gone back to their motel an hour or so earlier, so I made the lonely walk back to the multi-level parking garage and drove the nine-plus miles north from downtown Asheville to Weaverville, by myself.

By 9:30 P.M., I was stretched out on the couch, cradling a cup of tea. The calm was short-lived. At 11:00 P.M., the phone rang. "Mrs. Gates, your husband has suffered a Code Blue…Staff's brought him back (via the paddles), but we advise you to come in." They could tell me no more.

From the house, I notified Paul's family, and we arranged to meet at the hospital. As I drove back, I called my younger daughter for some much needed moral support. I faced the prospect of losing a partner I'd shared good times with, for the past many years, a man with whom I'd come to this region to begin our new life. And I had to drown out the haunting memories of earlier hospital experiences that ended badly.

"Do you want me to come?" my daughter asked. "Yes," I said. She immediately booked a flight to arrive the next day. She realized

I needed support, for she told me that throughout my earlier crises in life, I'd never asked for help.

When I arrived in the ICU, I noted the familiar machinery blinking, signaling the fact Paul was still with us. The rest of his family arrived, and we all sat in a mini-conference room where we awaited a doctor's official report.

When the hospital chaplain came by, offering assistance, I took her up on the offer and followed her to the chapel, where I fell into wracking sobs.

The emotion...the worry...the uncertain future had all welled up within and spilled out.

How odd: We'd come to Asheville for a less hectic life; Paul had driven all over the United States and foreign countries, as a big rig operator who'd won top awards in trucking, and now he'd been taken out on a mountain road by a twelve-year-old girl.

It would get crazier in the days and weeks ahead.

Quagmire

The next morning I picked up my daughter at the airport, and we went immediately to the hospital, where Paul was assigned to a room in Intensive Care Unit. Along the way, I prepared her for what she'd see. Instead of the vibrant individual who evidenced an irascible wit, I told her to expect a drawn and unresponsive man now kept alive by machinery.

I'd already learned that Paul suffered the Code Blue when his lungs shut down, following his choking due to the swelling in his throat. That situation precipitated his heart attack. The hospital characterized the anoxic period, the time when no oxygen went to his brain, as "brief."

Haunted by the scene the day before, when nurses noted his swollen tongue, I wondered if anyone had ordered steroids to cut down on the swelling or whether a doctor had considered intubation. I wondered, too: Was that swelling just a time-bomb ticking, with the inevitable result that he choked?

When my daughter and I left the hospital wing, I saw one of the nurses who'd been assigned to him on that earlier day shift call out: "Oh, hi...I heard about your husband's Code Blue. Wow, he was lucky a nurse was nearby who noted it so fast."

"Lucky"? I thought to myself: He would have been "lucky" if someone had taken steps to counter the swelling that nurses had noted earlier. He would have been "lucky" if he'd been assigned to the Intensive Care Unit from the git-go?

Over the next few days, Paul remained in ICU, swaddled in warm towels and heated blankets to keep him warm. My daughter made the observation that, lying there, with the white turban towel wrapped around his head, he looked like that beloved, extra-terrestrial movie creature, ET.

Nurses came in, periodically, to assess how he was doing, during which time they stopped the flow of Propofol, a milky-looking sedative. He'd awaken, mumble some response to one of their questions, and then they re-opened the valve to resume the drip. Off he'd go again into that induced coma state.

A team of doctors came and went: He had a cardiologist because he'd had a heart attack, a pulmonary person because he developed a pneumonia, and all sorts of other specialists. In the ICU, I never saw our neurosurgeon, although I knew he was kept in the loop.

We continued to hold court in his room, mostly standing, switching out the few chairs, while friends dropped in, periodically, making it past the "Relatives Only" ICU policy.

Four days later, Paul was assigned to a step-down room again, and my original team of family supporters left to resume their faraway lives.

Paul's sisters had flown in from Arkansas, and with their arrival, I directed my energy to other things of a pressing nature. In the hospital dining room, I met with North Carolina lawyers who gave me their professional opinion as to what legal route we could pursue against the uncle who'd allowed the girl to drive.

They examined our car insurance policies; they looked at the police report of the accident; they researched state law and how it might apply to us, a Rhode Island couple who lived part-time, in North Carolina.

In the meantime, a television reporter called: "We've heard there was an accident involving your husband being hit on a mountain road by a twelve year old girl," the reporter said. The girl's uncle had described the accident as "no big deal." He suggested there were only minor injuries.

With that, I became enraged and agreed to be interviewed, providing camera technicians blacked me out. I didn't know the party responsible, and I was already gearing up for an uphill battle with medical staff who were suggesting Paul would be ready to go home soon.

I didn't need more trouble.

But I was going to set the record straight: This was a serious accident in which Paul suffered a broken neck and attending neurological damage. We felt it an egregious wrong that the uncle allowed the child to drive the truck and even more insulting that he now characterized the accident as "no big deal."

The hospital allowed the interview to be taped in one of their first-floor conference rooms. My interview hit the air that night during the 6:00 o'clock news.

Below is Paul in ICU, in an induced coma, following his choking on post-surgical swelling. This set off a domino effect whereby his lungs shut down, precipitating a heart attack and death.

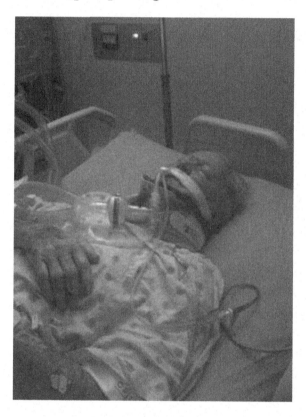

He's "Bonkers" and I'm Terrified

One morning Paul greeted my arrival by pointing to the television, saying: "See that man up there? He was here this morning, meeting with me." I glanced at the screen to see Sanjay Gupta, CNN's medical expert. "Sanjay Gupta was here?" I asked. "Yes," he replied, "we had a long discussion."

Later, a cafeteria staffer came into the room, asking: "Sir, do you have your meal selection sheet finished?" Paul looked at me and said, "Honey, what do you think? Do we want to stay another night?" (as if we were at a Bed 'n Breakfast, needing to tell proprietors if we were going to extend our stay).

I feared Paul was completely crazy.

At one point, he told me about an incident where men in white coats were beating on his chest. He felt they were trying to rob him. He went on to say the assault took place in a long, glass box that had a hole for air; the men were outside, trying to get at him. I surmised he was reliving the Code Blue event when the triage group worked to resuscitate him.

On another day, he sat in the hospital side chair, playing with the remote control that raised and lowered his bed. "Colleen, when did we get this bed?" he asked.

On yet another occasion he asked: "Are we in the little house we had on Jefferson Boulevard?" He was referring to a home in Rhode Island where he had lived forty years before we met.

I registered my concerns about his deteriorated mental state, in messages to the doctor and his staff, but no one from the hospital came in to talk to me. Oh, they kept telling me someone would, but that never happened. My fears mounted.

On the day my daughter was to return home, I dropped her off at the front of the hospital, so she could say goodbye to Paul, while I parked. The plan was for me to come in, retrieve her, and we'd go to the airport.

As I came across the threshold of Paul's room, I heard the neurosurgeon say, "Well, maybe we'll have to give her some Valium, to calm her down." My daughter's jaw dropped.

"What'd you say?" I asked as I entered.

"Your daughter said you're very worried about your husband's mental state, and I said maybe we should give you something to calm you down," he responded somewhat sheepishly.

I let his remark go. I needed to choose my battles.

As he was leaving, he announced that Paul would be discharged at any time. I protested, saying he wasn't ready. "Mrs. Gates (that's not my name)," he said, "hospitals are for sick people and your husband's no longer sick."

No, I thought, he's not sick…he's just mentally deranged. You fixed him physically and destroyed his mind, in the process.

He then told me he'd be turning Paul over to "someone in your brother's field—a neurologist." (Hoping to insure a bond of sorts, I'd once told him that my brother was a neurologist.)

Later that day, the neurologist came to our room. A bespectacled guy of serious demeanor, seemingly devoid of personality, he sat in the corner chair of Paul's room, and talked at me, delivering the spiel I'm sure he's given on countless other occasions: "There's no way of determining how much your husband will recover mentally."

When I asked if his mental situation could have resulted from the anoxic event, he said, "Much of his mental deterioration had probably already been in the works, by virtue of his age."

So, there it was: The neurologist suggested my seriously befuddled mate suffered from something that was most likely happening, anyway.

Were they working on a "preexisting condition" defense? I wondered.

What that neurologist didn't know–and never asked–is that Paul had a thorough physical each year in Rhode Island. Our primary care provider would attest to his soundness of body and mind. No deterioration had ever been noted.

In addition, before Paul's surgery, he was perfectly fit, mentally. In the day immediately following surgery, he was clear. His confusion had come on the heels of the Code Blue and the anoxic event.

In my mind, hospital staff were circling the wagons and disavowing responsibility. They were already making the case that his problems were simply the natural course of aging and had nothing to do with poor medical judgments or malpractice.

The bonfire was building within me.

At War

Nearly hysterical with fear, I sought advice from everyone I knew. The consensus? "Make sure Paul gets a psych-neuro evaluation and an Electroencephalogram (EEG) before the hospital discharges him."

I left a message at the neurosurgeon's office that I wanted those tests done before Paul Gates was discharged.

The next morning I came into the hospital room to find a young woman administering a test, via a machine on wheels. She asked Paul a series of questions for approximately forty minutes and made periodic notations while I sat in a corner, observing. At the completion, she turned to me and mouthed the words: "Has he been saying things like this right along?"

Since his answers seemed crazy, I knew what she meant. I nodded "Yes," and I asked her to record her observations, along with her official findings, to confirm what I'd been noting over the last several days. She said she would.

Then the phone rang. It was the neurosurgeon. He said he'd just ducked out of surgery to let me know Paul was ready to go home. He'd be discharged that day.

"No...I don't think so," I said confidently. "Paul's not ready to go home. He's being given the psych-neuro evaluation now."

"On whose authority?" the doctor asked.

When I answered, "Mine," he burst out laughing.

It was then that I lost all composure. I could no longer put up with such disrespect.

"You're laughing at me? How dare you? You think all of this is funny, while I'm crazy with worry and fear that you've fixed my husband, physically, only to destroy his mind, in the process."

"I've been putting up with your arrogance for weeks now, and I don't plan on doing it one more minute. You tell the hospital to send someone else to me, for I'm not talking to you from this point forward."

The line was drawn. I was at war with the hospital and with this cocky surgeon.

At that, I dropped the phone and ducked into Paul's bathroom, shut the door, and doubled over, sobbing. All the pent-up fears came out; I could hold back no more.

Some moments later, I went to the sink, splashed water on my face, straightened my outfit, and reentered the room. The neurosurgeon and a nurse were waiting.

"I told you I'd not speak to you; I've had it with you. You've dismissed my husband and me from the beginning, and I'm not putting up with your arrogance one more minute."

He tried to explain. "I wasn't laughing at you. It's just that I've never had a patient tell me she'd ordered tests before."

"Well, you've never dealt with me before," I shot back. "And I want those tests done before any talk about Paul's discharge."

Everything I thought but hadn't said came rushing out. "You don't know that man in that bed over there…you don't know what type of person he is. But he's certainly nothing like the man I came in with. I want to know what happened that night of the Code

Blue. How long was he anoxic? What's 'brief?'"(the hospital's characterization of the event).

"Whose idea was it to assign this patient who'd just endured a nine-hour surgery you characterized as 'most difficult' to a step-down room, instead of ICU?"

"Finally, when nurses noted his tongue swelling, was anything done to counter it (as in administer steroids or intubate)? Was a doctor brought in to evaluate?"

When I pressed for an answer, the neurologist said: "I'm not responsible for what staff does on the floor."

"Who assigned him to a step-down room, from the beginning?" I reiterated.

The third time I asked, he finally acknowledged that room assignment was his decision.

"Doctor, you've got a lot to learn from your patients. Just for the record, I divorced one husband and buried two more, before you were even out of medical school."

I brought up his Valium comment, too, saying I'd taken offense, noting: "The days are over, doctor, when male physicians seek to quiet a concerned woman with drugs."

"I was just trying to lighten a difficult situation," he said.

"For whom? Do you really believe your joking is going to lighten a concern I have about my husband's mental condition?"

"No, doctor, the appropriate response concerning your inappropriate remark is: 'I'm sorry.'"

When he didn't respond, I drove the point home by slowly mouthing the two words. He finally apologized.

I then told him that I expected the hospital to develop a new game plan, for Paul wasn't merely going home. I wanted Paul assigned to a rehabilitation center where they'd ascertain the degree of his mental damage.

"If the hospital had ever bothered to discuss a discharge plan with me," I said, "they'd have learned that I have MS and I'm incapable of providing for him at home."

To this day, I believe that information was the critical piece they had never considered—my inability to be the sole care provider for my partner. I'd removed the hospital's automatic designation of me as caregiver.

Paul was transferred to a nearby rehabilitation facility the next day.

I had achieved my immediate goal of buying time—as well as a second medical assessment of Paul by an objective medical authority.

Long Road to Recovery

After a twelve day hospitalization, Paul began the second stage of his recovery at a nearby rehabilitation center.

Once he was settled in a room, I met privately with the social worker to express my fears that the hospital had fixed Paul, physically, only to deliver to me a person who'd lost his mind. I was terrified for what the future would bring.

"We'll see how he is over the next several days," the social worker said, after listening intently to what I had to say.

He told me what the hospital should have told me but never did: Paul's mental deterioration could be the product of drug interaction (he was on fifteen medications); hospital psychosis (where a patient never sleeps and gets crazy); the anoxic episode (no oxygen to the brain, when he choked); or a combination of some or all.

He advised we rule out variables one by one, to see if he progressed.

At least, now, I felt I had a partner in this rehabilitation facility, one willing to hear my concerns and give me an active role in my partner's recovery—a role denied me at the hospital.

Paul and I agreed that he'd go off the mind-altering drugs, but continue those we considered essential. In the days ahead, I saw real improvement as Paul's mind became clearer. But it would be a long time before we were out of the woods.

Staff helped a shaky Paul with walking and doing self-maintenance tasks such as brushing his teeth and dressing himself. They assessed his ability to recall items in a series and compute simple mathematical equations. They gave us hope that skills in these areas might improve over time.

After five days as in-patient, Paul was discharged with an outpatient plan for therapy to continue in three-times-weekly sessions. In the meantime, to counteract his pain, I pumped him full of ibuprofen. We took short walks to increase his endurance.

Finally, when he was given the "All clear" sign by doctors, I packed a couple of suitcases and shut down our winter home in North Carolina. We flew home to Rhode Island, while a friend drove our car the seven hundred-plus miles from Asheville. When she arrived, we hosted her for a few-days respite; I drove her around to tourist favorites; and then we paid for her ticket back to North Carolina, via plane.

Our first medical visit in Rhode Island was to our general practitioner who checked Paul overall, while I filled him in on events that transpired.

Over the next several weeks, I brought Paul to physical therapy three times a week, and we got him set up with a neurologist whom he saw regularly. He wore the hard collar throughout the hot summer months.

The weakness in his arm got better, and he got stronger.

The neurologist recommended a memory specialist to determine the nature and severity of Paul's memory loss. Specifically, we hoped to learn whether Paul's diminished recall was attributable to the accident and anoxic period.

But Paul no longer had the stamina he once had. He tired easily, took naps often, or had to sit down in the mere attempts at jobs he formerly did, easily. Anything that required fine motor skills presented a challenge, as he dropped items and became frustrated. Since he lost the capacity to recall items in sequence, I wrote everything down. I needed to put lists in prominent spots, hoping he'd remember to look at the lists.

All the while the medical bills arrived, to the tune of hundreds of thousands of dollars. The hospital, the surgeon, the rehabil- itation center kept sending bills for services, medicines, or pro- cedures, most of which confused and obfuscated. The bills were gibberish and we were awash in them.

When I called North Carolina's District Attorney's office, I dis- covered that the man at fault for the accident–the man who let the twelve-year-old drive– was merely charged with contributing to the delinquency of a minor and child abuse. He'd gotten away pretty much unscathed and was right in his first analysis: The accident was 'no big deal,' for him.

Oh, we recovered from that man's car insurer, but it was North Carolina's state-mandated liability minimum of $30,000 ($25,000 for Rhode Island). The amount fell far short of our actual dam- ages which were well over $500,000.

In the future, I'd make sure we had "underinsured insurance," to protect us in the event the other party had no insurance or the other driver's insurance was insufficient.

The late model car Paul was driving was a total loss, and we lost our lives as active, energetic, young seniors. Now our days were filled with doctor appointments, physical and occupational ther- apy sessions. We felt we'd been drop-kicked into a surreal, never- ending nightmare of horrific proportion.

But events had changed me. I'd become a strong patient ad- vocate, a woman no longer willing to acquiesce to unilateral deci- sions made by others, affecting us.

I'd get to test that resolve immediately.

Our "Out-of-Towners'"
Airline Disaster Story

S ince we were advised by doctors not to drive the seven hundred miles home for the fact a sudden stop in the car would
compromise Paul's newly-mended neck bones, I booked Paul and
me a flight on Continental Airlines, to get us home sooner. We
couldn't know at the time that the flight would present even more
risk.

• • •

"The Out-of-Towners" was a 1970 cinema hit starring Jack Lem-
mon and Sandy Dennis as George and Gwen Kellerman, a
couple from Twin Oaks, Ohio, in New York City for George's interview for a vice- president-for-marketing position with his company.

While there, they are confounded by a series of maddening
events: Their plane is detoured to another city; luggage is lost; and
because of lateness, they lose their reservations at the posh hotel where they booked a room. They're mugged, muddied (a cab
splashed them), and demoralized. Feeling supremely impotent,
George demands names of all who are indifferent or rude, wagging

his finger and threatening: "You're going to regret this. I've got your name and I'm reporting you to your boss." Nobody cared.

Paul and I endured our own "Out of Towners'" experience, but the setting wasn't a booming, indifferent metropolis, and the offenders weren't faceless strangers. They were the airline I booked for our flight home, Continental Airline, with one connection, in Newark, where there would be a layover time of 90 minutes.

While we sat at the gate in Newark for Providence, I noted departure times kept changing from 3:30 to 4...then 4:30...and 5.

Meanwhile, the airline made no announcements, and people milled around. By 5:30, Paul was beginning to show serious signs of distress. At that point, I insisted on speaking with a manager.

I pointed out Paul (the one with the Aspen collar bracing his neck) and shared my concern: Our flight had been delayed many times; we'd been moved to four different gates; new flights kept arriving and leaving all around us; Paul could not sit for this long, and there was nowhere for him to lie down.

The airline manager said: "There's no plane for Providence—we're searching for one now." I said, "Just tell us when you think we'll be able to get us out of here," and he answered, "It could be 11 tonight and we could still have no plane."

I told him that his answer was unacceptable.

I also told him we'd need to get our bag, get a room in Newark, and take a bus to Rhode Island in the morning. He advised me that the airline would not compensate us for the room and directed us to the baggage-claim area, an entire corridor length away and down one level. He offered no other assistance.

A third of the way, when Paul floundered, I flagged a porter wheeling an empty wheelchair and commandeered them. He brought us to a bank of baggage clerks to retrieve our bag.

After some moments, a clerk announced: "Your bag is already loaded on the plane to Providence. It's on the tarmac now, ready to leave." I said, "What? It can't be...we just left there. The manager told me there might not even be a plane by 11 tonight."

I panicked: "My husband's medications are in that bag and he needs them." I had taken out only the number he would need for the day, fearing if I carried more, the airline would confiscate them.

A snippy clerk commented: "Why, on earth, would you pack medication in a checked bag?" I sucked in my response and asked that they hold the plane. What happened next was a litany of horror.

The young woman the airline sent with the wheelchair took two steps to my five, despite my prompting to "Please hurry." Ramps were far longer than other routes; we waited for a slow elevator to bring us up a level; and we headed back through security checkpoints. One monitor who felt we were rudely jumping the line barked: "If you want to make a flight, get here EARLY. You don't even have your documents ready." (In my panic, I forgot we had to do this again.) To punish us, she slow-scanned our documents, holding us up longer.

As we went again through the body-scanning machine, Paul was pulled aside and ordered out of the wheelchair, to be screened individually. He tried to balance himself as he removed his shoes (there were no chairs). When I approached him to help, they waved me away. It was brutal.

We finally made the long journey back down the corridor to discover no sign telling us where the Providence flight was (new flights were on the boards). I called out to airline personnel: "Does anyone know where the Providence flight is?" Silence.

In desperation, we went out a door to a plane sitting on the tarmac, but we were signaled away; it was not our flight. A mechanic motioned us to the other side. We went back into the terminal and pushed through a new crowd swelling the exit.

The porter rolled Paul's wheelchair out the opposite gate and across the concrete expanse to the elusive Providence plane. He stopped at the base of the stairs. As if in final assault, Paul would now have to mount that flight of stairs.

Once we were inside and seated, a man across the aisle said: "What happened? We thought you left" (he was one of five of us who voiced our concerns to management, earlier). I told him we went for our bag only to learn they'd gotten a plane and our bag was loaded. We told him the uphill battle we'd endured getting back.

At that moment, a young woman across the aisle, in the seat in front of him, turned to face me full-on and screamed, "Oh, for God sakes, it was three fucking hours. Will you shut the fuck up!"

It was then I became a 21st Century George Kellerman of "The Out-of-Towners." In no uncertain terms, I told her what I thought of her and her filthy language. She was simply the final insult in a day we'd borne far too much misery and degradation.

What did all this teach me? In the future, I'll read customer reviews of airlines on the Internet and make airline accountability the determinant for how we choose carriers. And for those who are older or infirm, realize: The way some airline carriers treat their customers may become more than inconvenience; it may become a matter of life or death.

In other words, you might want to drive (or get another to drive you).

An Angel Appears

When Paul and I arrived back in Rhode Island that spring, I was at one of my lowest points. I'd just come off battling everyone: lawyers in North Carolina were disinclined to take our case; hospital representatives and doctors clamored for money; the flight had been a disaster; we'd come home to a caved-in swimming pool due to floods and unusual rains that spring.

My nerves were raw. I felt alone in a sea of disaster.

To this day, I cannot believe what happened next: On a brutally hot day in July, I suggested we go to the Wickford Art Festival, an every year event that we'd not attended for years. In and of itself, such a plan was insane, for I steer clear of crowds (and this event is always packed), and Paul wore a hard neck collar which meant he was more uncomfortable in the searing heat.

No matter—We went.

While walking through the crowd, I heard a woman call out: "Hello Colleen." It was a woman with whom I'd taught in the same school for nineteen years. Helene was accompanied by her husband, Joel, a noted lawyer in our state, one with whom I was most familiar for his successful handling of a case involving a policeman sentenced for a murder that he'd never committed. The wrongfully convicted former police officer had recently been released.

They asked us what happened and I told them. I also told them that I was going to call insurance companies the following Monday to accept whatever we could get, to end the punishing rounds of calls from everyone to whom we supposedly owed money. Joel advised me not to do that...recommended I call him to set up a time and place to meet and discuss options. He pressed his business card into my hand.

Because of that chance meeting, Paul and I ultimately recovered from the other party's insurer and our insurance companies.

What did I learn throughout the two year process of depositions and ultimate negotiated settlement? Based upon the circumstances of each case, the lawyer can negotiate with the hospital and other medical providers to accept a reduced payment, with the remaining balance forgiven.

I would have never known to negotiate the amount...wouldn't have even known what I could offer. Lawyers do know, if their practice involves dealing with insurance companies.

That chance meeting (or was it?) that day in the little village of Wickford, Rhode Island, saved Paul and me in extraordinary ways: we had a potent and knowledgeable advocate; we were blessedly free from harassing phone calls (all stopped as soon as I stated that I had a lawyer).

Then, too, we recovered... at least financially.

I continue to be amazed that, at what I consider the darkest moments of my life, someone stepped into the breach and saved me. I hardly think they are accidents of life. I prefer to see these special people as angels.

Our attorney, Joel Chase, of Warwick, Rhode Island, is one.

Regrouping and Final Decision-Making

In the first year post-accident, in Rhode Island, I continued taking Paul to physical therapy three times a week, and we kept regular appointments with his primary care doctor and his Rhode Island neurologist. We signed Paul on, too, with Rhode Island Hospital's Memory Clinic, where they monitored memory changes that might develop in one who'd had a brain injury.

It was a grueling schedule.

And sometime in that period of "awful," I got a call from his Asheville neurosurgeon, the one who had been so arrogant. I don't know why to this day. Maybe a hospital administrator directed that doctor to reach out and apologize (fearing a lawsuit), since I had written of his callous behavior to his superiors, or maybe—just maybe—he wanted to make things right, after all.

He said he was sorry...that when he told me he "knew cancer in his own right" (I'd shared with him the fact I'd had breast cancer), he was referencing his own struggle, for his wife was battling cancer at the time he met us. I asked if he had children and he said, "Yes, five little ones." I told him I was sorry for his situation and wished him and his wife a good result.

We ended our conversation at that point, but to this day, I hope I was instrumental in teaching him the importance of communicating better with patients and their families.

When we returned in January, to Asheville, I began writing articles for the *Mountain Express,* a much-respected magazine in the mountains of North Carolina, similar to the alternative Rhode Island newspaper, the *Providence Phoenix.* My column, "Asheville Under Glass," purported to analyze life in this quirky little town from the perspective of an older, retirement-age person. At the same time, I continued writing for our Rhode Island state newspaper, the Pulitzer-Prize-winning *Providence Journal,* in Rhode Island.

But the trips back and forth were becoming more difficult. What normally had been problematic (juggling two homes) now posed daunting problems, since I handled more of the tasks.

With that realization, I determined that we needed to make a decision: Which state would we live in, permanently—North Carolina or Rhode Island?

Paul and I discussed it thoroughly.

In the year since the accident, I saw Paul frequently bored with life in our townhome. He no longer went to the gym (in a nearby separate building of our complex), and he failed to ride his bike into the hills. It was clear to me that life as we knew it had changed. He didn't have the same energy.

In Rhode Island, we considered the fact we both can ride bikes for a good part of the year; we have wonderful bike trails carved out of old railroad beds, designated for those of us who love the sport; they're reasonably flat so I (a person with a mild form of multiple sclerosis) can ride long stretches, with little difficulty.

When we tire of Rhode Island's bike trails, we access those in nearby Massachusetts, on the Cape, following the ever-resplendent National Seashore.

In Asheville, bike riding mandates one "share the road," a requirement we were never comfortable with, as roadways wind along mountain passes, necessitating tricky maneuvering, even for cars. Then, too, the ascents are steep. I can go distance...just not uphill where upper leg strength is required.

We discussed whether it would bother us to never be near the ocean again, and we both determined that such a loss would be too great. The seven hour trek to the shores of North Carolina posed too far a distance. And because I was born in "The Ocean State," Rhode Island, I knew I couldn't permanently trade the sea for the mountains. Nor could I adjust to the long flat stretches of beaches in the Carolinas or Florida.

We love the character of the New England coastline, with its inlets... marshes...little harbors that provide a panoramic view at every turn.

Finally, too, Paul needed a yard—the same yard he spent ten hours or so a day, in the growing season, cutting grass, pruning, raking, and keeping all in shape. He'd go from garage, out to the pool, monitoring and checking, filling bird feeders, fishing an errant-but-still-alive chipmunk who'd taken a wrong turn too close to the pool.

Yes, these duties kept him motivated, and I recognized this. He would never be a townhome kind of person whose activity revolved around an eighteen hundred foot inner living space, with its own, carefully regulated small plot of land.

And then, too, there was my budding writing career. Living in two regions proved problematic in that I failed to get properly rooted in either. My literary career had already suffered.

When I took on a position as host for monthly presentations of the Association of Rhode Island Authors (ARIA), I renamed the event "Lively Literati" and created kicky theme-based monthly discussion topics, but then I had to quit that position, shortly after Christmas. Just as I was building momentum, I had to stop and restart the engine in Asheville.

It was clear: I needed consistency—at least in the period of establishing my writing and guest-speaking credentials.

But before we made any real final decision regarding permanent residence, we determined to thank our community for the love they'd shown, during our medical crisis. As such, I planned and hosted Paul's 70th birthday party, a catered event held at our townhome community's clubhouse. The following is my address to our community, a "roast" of Paul, highlighting the gala event–one I seriously doubted we'd ever see just one year before.

Paul Wesley Gates on the Unexpected Event of His Turning 70!

To Our Hamburg Crossing Community:

Born on March 1, 1941, in the rural splotch of Arkansas known as "the Bottoms" (the high uppy-ups didn't live there), Paul Wesley Gates lived an almost Davy Crockett kind of life. He was the oldest of five kids and the family was anything but rich. Out of necessity, he learned to hunt and fish so they could eat.

How would this factor as important in his life? Many years later, he'd go on to lead his National Guard company, as Sergeant First Class. As an expert marksman, he took his crack shooting team to Arkansas every year to compete nationally, against teams all over the country. One year they came in third in the nation. All that practice as a boy came in "real handy." When one has to shoot for his supper, he becomes good—or goes hungry.

Flash forward to Paul's young adult years when he high-tailed it all over the country, as an independent owner-operator of a big rig, transporting household furniture. When I asked in later years, "Have you been to such-and-such a place?" Paul simply answered: "I been by it."

It took me a while to figure out he'd never been TO anywhere--just passed it in a blur on the "superslab," as he colorfully called the nation's highways. He hired men, all over this country, too, as loaders, unloaders, and drivers; he knew the laws of every state (and how to skirt them); he'd been in a couple of jails for non-compliance....which is all the more interesting for how that would play out in his next professional "gig" in life.

When he tired of trucking (and noted fellow truckers popping up in the obituaries in their 50's and 60's), Paul stepped off the rig and became an officer in Rhode Island's Department of Corrections. He did well there, too, for he lacked the hair-trigger temper that derailed others. The inmates respected him, and he returned the favor in that he honored the fact many simply went off-road for a while.

Paul always recognized: Everyone's journey in this life is different. Certainly, no one knew that better than he. The man who'd been disinvited from school, in the eleventh grade, after he accidentally set the woods on fire, when he sought a smoke break with a friend, took a many-year path to learn life's lessons.

While in the military and in Corrections, he got his GED and associate's degree.

In life, he earned many more degrees.

In a way, he should have a doctorate, for he was a journeyman roofer (when he was only 18 years old); he did two stints of the service (in the Navy and the Army); he completed a career as a National Guardsman; he was a thirty year owner-operator of his own trucking company and spent eighteen years as Correctional Officer.

As to recent glory: Paul defied death last year following his near-fatal accident on that mountain road, when he was hit by a twelve year old girl. It took months for him to regain strength but experts say: "If he hadn't been in the prime condition he was, he wouldn't have had such a productive outcome."

It wasn't the first time he cheated the Grim Reaper. Some years ago, I saved him when I had to haul him up out of his seat at the dining table, where he choked on the steak I'd prepared. I began the pumping action of the Heimlich (he always calls it "the Hemlock"), causing him to cough up the food plug stuck in his throat.

Another time, I flew out the door to lift a motorcycle off him, just like the famous mother who lifted a car off her child, due to her adrenaline rush. I'd heard the Hruuummmppp, when Paul lost his balance and saw the bike come crashing down on him, pinning him beneath.

This mountain episode was the third, and I warned him: "You've used up all your passes."

Today is not simply a celebration of Paul's 70th (tho' that is momentous). It's also a "Thank you," to you all, our community, for your unceasing support of us throughout this ordeal. We couldn't imagine another community where folks send gift cards, pay visits, make meals, and even give the caregiver (me) a wonderful spa gift.

Then, too, there was that selfless act by one of you (Joyce) who drove our car the seven hundred miles up, from Asheville to Rhode Island, so we could fly home.

In any case, we love you all and have considered ourselves blessed with good fortune for having you in our lives. We have never ceased to marvel that just when something seemed so dark and ominous, you kept us buoyed.

We'll be forever grateful, Hamburg Crossing community.

Hope Out of Ashes: *Grandpa* and the *Truck* Books

Throughout my life, I have learned to get back on the metaphorical horse, following a major fall. Oh, not right away, of course, for one needs time to process and recover. But past experiences have taught me: No one would fix my problems; I'd need to be the one to do it. It was either that or retreat to a corner and lick my wounds which, frankly, isn't my style.

Our formerly active lifestyle had changed almost overnight, and we were forced to endure significant downtime to allow Paul's body to heal. No medical professionals could tell us, either, if he'd significantly improve.

During that first summer, when our three, out-of-state grandkids came to visit in Rhode Island, I began telling them Paul's trucking adventures, and then, on each successive visit, they begged me to tell them another *Grandpa and the Truck* story.

As a teacher, I thought the stories great vehicles for teaching important life lessons. Each of his stories took place in a different state, so I could bring out regional differences, and I built up suspenseful events, telling them about the life of a long-haul trucker and how big rig drivers communicate with each other via their CB radios.

One day our littlest one rolled his toy big rig over the hardwood floor saying "Breaker...breaker..1..9. Any smokies up ahead on the superslab?" Since he was mimicking the trucker talk I'd used in the stories, referring to the CB radio, police, and highways, I knew I was onto something. I knew, too, that the stories appealed across different age brackets (our littlest one was three years younger than his twin brothers who also liked the stories).

As a grandmother, I frequently noted that many children's stories were warm and fuzzy, but they lacked substance.

The teacher in me got to work.

I mapped out story lines for each *Grandpa and the Truck* book, sketched pictures I thought would work, created a page of questions and trucking terms to go with each story, added maps, tables of contents, and bubbles of interesting facts.

Next, we went on a hunt to find our illustrator.

Together, Paul and I visited various western North Carolina art schools and spoke to others who might know an artist looking for freelance work. We put up flyers at AB Tech and Warren Wilson College, saying, "Wanted: Illustrator of children's book series."

At Asheville's AB Tech, I'd been successful hiring student help, when I needed a tech tutor for the three years I wrote a blog (I put my ad for a student tutor on AB Tech's student notices board). My two hires, Andrew Plyler and Jess Jacobs, of Asheville, were instrumental in helping me achieve the rudiments of blogging. Both were excellent and a tribute to the product AB Tech produced.

Finally, in the River Arts District, in Asheville, a person recommended the woman who became our artist. In the weeks ahead, we met with Dana Irwin to exchange ideas. We brought her out to the truck dealership, Wilson Trucking, in Canton, to familiarize her with the big rigs, to help in her drawing and eventual painting.

We went to her home, weekly, in the Montford section, of Asheville, and pored over the work, approving or explaining why changes were necessary. She did the necessary alterations, and I OK'd the final product.

In this fashion, we completed two *Grandpa and the Truck* books (two stories in each). Each story was set in a different geographic location. "We Teach Geography...and a Whole Lot More" became our tag line. Our stories were about nature (storms and weather's impact on the big rigs), historical events (hurricane Camille and Woodstock Music Festival); regional differences, life lessons.

Our plan was to have young readers follow the big rig across America, giving them other-than-GPS-knowledge of our great country.

The biggest international trucking association, OOIDA, and Women In Trucking (WIT) endorsed our products and gave us quotes for the back of our books. We established our own website to explain our mission and sell our books and we tried to get the word out.

But we'd discover: self-publishing children's books is difficult indeed: First, there's the matter of investment. Since we're not artists, we expended $3,000 on illustrations before our books were out the gate, a cost not borne by authors who solely write words or even add photos to the work.

Next, we faced the problem all authors face of how to get eyes on the product. Over the next two years, I approached the trucking industry on multiple occasions, only to be met with indifference.

I couldn't fathom industry disinterest in a children's book series which was the first of its kind, one that glorified truckers and the hard job they do every day, while the stories taught children important lessons.

I sought entry into Cracker Barrel's varied market in that they tout their commitment to distinctly American products. To my mind, what's more "American" than children's books based on those who delivered their products...American truckers and their big rigs?

Despite my efforts, I couldn't get through their corporate door.

I wrote to Atlas Van Lines (Paul was named a member of their Elite Fleet for his driving expertise and his many-year career without incident or accident), suggesting they align with us, since the industry predicts a loss of drivers in the years ahead, if they can't attract good drivers.

I believed stories heralding the career experiences of one of the industry's best would be a shot in the arm for trucking.

They had no interest.

Finally, when I was convinced truck companies wouldn't be our allies, I sought support from educators and last year, at an educational collaborative, I met a librarian coordinator who was greatly impressed with our books.

He told me there's a dearth of books offering Table of Contents, vocabulary, and questions, along with story and illustrations. He applauded our product.

With that, we agreed to combine forces. He'd test-drive our books, and we'd do a presentation at two of the town's schools where he was a librarian.

In that spring, before a two hundred child audience comprised of kindergarten through sixth graders, I ran my PowerPoint presentation. It began with a kicky song, describing a big rig hurtling down a mountain road, with sparks flying and wheels smoking. The driver fears wiping out the town below, since the truck carries explosive nitro. My audience of little ones swayed to the beat.

Then, I described a long-haul trucker's life: why he's like a turtle (a trucker carries his house—cab—around with him); distances these truckers go; what state they can't go to; truck stops;

CB radios, weigh stations (they're not designed to weed out fat truckers).

The show at the first school went spectacularly, for they provided the promised audio-visual equipment. The kids were riveted and asked the trucker questions. At the end, with signage I provided, they physically acted out our geography lesson in response to my prompts (signifying the states the trucker went to—and which one he did not).

Our show at the second school presented serious challenges in that school administrators failed to provide the audio-visual equipment promised, so the kicky beginning song...bloodhounds howling...hurricane roaring would not be heard. The microphones weren't working either, presenting another problem.

Whereas I was initially told I'd be wearing a mike (thus freeing my hands to control the PowerPoint), I now had to sit at the laptop and put the mike next to the speaker on my computer in order to transmit sound. This all made me nervous, indeed, for I'm not skilled in technological workings. I had to remain tethered to my computer, which disallowed me from walking about, engaging with my young audience.

I became flustered in a process that was unfamiliar to me in a cafeteria that was sweltering. School administrators offered no help but sat back and watched me flounder.

Even so, despite all of the problems, the students were spectacular. Another large audience (two hundred and fifty kids), they were attentive and engaged, throughout.

These assemblies confirmed what I know: *Grandpa and the Truck* books are a vehicle for exciting teaching.

What else did I learn? Not to rely on others. When I present, I must control the equipment or bring a flash drive to use with a school's computer, aligned with their system. Preferably, I should bring all my own equipment.

In the end, I am stunned at the realization that the birth of the *Grandpa and the Truck* books came about due to our profound tragedy in Asheville. When one door closes, another opens.

But one must walk through that door.

P.S. We have 6-8 more *Grandpa and the Truck* books in the series that we plan to publish.

Our *Grandpa and the Truck* (Books 1 and 2) are available at the website we manage (grandpaandthetruck.com). We will sign and personalize the book(s), if you–as buyer– state how you want the wording, in "instructions," on the payment site.

Dry Run at Sale

In full disclosure mode, I'll say upfront: I was a highly success-ful realtor for eight years, in Rhode Island, on the heels of my thirty year career as teacher. Both careers involve teaching. In one, I taught English and Journalism to secondary students. As realtor, I taught my clients how to buy and sell homes successfully.

Throughout my second career, all clients either met me at Open Houses and hired my services from that meeting or were referred to me by friends. Only twice did a real estate company with whom I aligned give me a referral, a situation where the of-fice assigns a realtor a client who's expressed interest in buying or selling. Ironically, the company with whom I was aligned longest gave me no referrals.

In other words, my reputation and work ethic got me clients.

My background and experience as realtor figured prominently in what would happen when we bought and sold our townhome in Weaverville, North Carolina.

As a realtor, I know that houses that sell quickly share the same basic traits: good floor plan; modernized kitchens and baths; mut-ed Pottery Barn-type colors on walls; an uncluttered visual field; updated furniture. Homes that don't sell look old and tired, with patterned wallpaper and printed upholstery or slipcovers (unless sellers are truly going for the vintage look), but they should know in advance: If they go that route, their buyer market will be severely limited. Yes, some buyers thrill to the discovery a home has shag green carpeting or kitchen pine cabinetry of the 60's (especially in Asheville), but those buyers are the decided exception.

I recall a townhome in our Hamburg Crossing complex, hanging on the market for the longest time, despite it being the "Sell-in-a-New-York-Minute, one-level Canterbury." It came with a lovely landscaped lot. What held it back? Whole walls painted flaming coral. Buyers apparently came to Open Houses and said "Ouch!" They couldn't get past the howling hues, and the unit found no suitors. When the owner finally painted the walls a neutral shade, it sold.

Is questionable physical location of a unit in a community a detriment to sale? Not if handled correctly. For instance, if the unit fronts a retaining wall or berm, a wise realtor can pose that position as one that insures privacy: the unit will never endure the frequent foot traffic of walkers who generally seek circular, inner paths. A high wall might offer a sense of security and privacy.

With a realtor's eye for eventual possibility of selling, I determined preferences when we bought: I fought the builder on kitchen counter granite selection (he wanted to use one with a green vein running through it that he'd installed in several units). I wanted black granite with amber vein, to pick up on the similar color of maple cabinetry and warm, butterscotch oak floors (also my choice).

When we ordered hardwood floors, I asked the floor company that installed most floors in our complex about customer preference. Did they prefer "glued-down" or "floating"? I was told that many found floating floors disconcerting for the hollow sound footfalls make, when a person walks on them. With that, we opted for glued-down, hardwood floors. (Our units were built on slabs.)

But I knew to ask the questions that would make decision-making easier and more productive.

I learned, first-hand, the wisdom of buying a townhome in a community that's completely built, for a potential buyer can't merely go by the footprint or the builder's design to understand how the unit will look in actuality.

For instance, if your unit is going to be feet away from an eight-foot retaining wall, will you find that claustrophobic? Will it annoy you that your unit is on the inner track where everyone walks dogs, and will it bother you when some residents allow their pets to relieve themselves on the patch of grass nearest you, because in effect, it's not your land (it's communal property belonging to the townhome community)?

Will your unit be the one with the large grey metal utility boxes that residents are not allowed to camouflage with plants or greenery, lest they not be readily accessible?

Will yours be the unit right behind a bank of mailboxes, insuring you have cars stopping in front of your townhome all day and night, the glare from their headlights pouring through your windows?

You'll not realize many factors, if you buy at earlier stages of construction. We found it preferable to buy once we saw the community up and running.

Following the boom market, eleven years ago (when we bought), whole townhome communities in the general region of Asheville went bankrupt because they couldn't find buyers (the market flipped) or buyers couldn't get financing (tougher to get financing for condos/townhomes, since plurality of ownership means more risk for financing institutions). Those situations prompted me to wonder about the buyers who bought first: Did those incompletely occupied communities result in residents having to absorb higher costs of trash collecting, snow removal, landscaping? In other words, did their HOA (Homeowners' Association) fee go up?

I knew to ask if older townhome communities had flush capital fund reserves, money earmarked for eventual major repairs, new roofs, future exterior painting of complex, septic system upgrade (if applies). It's surprising how few buyers ask to see this vital information.

As realtor, I noted the marketing trend whereby builders first sell the outer perimeter of homes in a new development and then fill in inner tracks, with houses later. What happens? Initial purchasers don't realize how their visual field will be affected until the community's complete. If owners are irate when their view is disrupted, there's little for them to do but sell. After all, they saw the builder's model and as we all know: The Devil's in the details.

We decided a year before we actually sold that we'd test the waters and put our townhome on the market. That year had seen several other townhomes go on the market, with some lingering for months. At some points, there'd been as many as eight or nine "For Sale," concurrently. We wanted to avoid the hot selling season of April-October.

With that, in January, I stuck a "For Sale by Owner" sign in the window and promptly forgot it was there.

One night some weeks later, we were at the clubhouse on a Friday night, socializing with members of our community. My cell phone rang. A buyer wanted to see our unit the next morning at 10:00 AM.

She arrived with her daughter and the daughter's partner. The mother had a home in Ohio that she shared with her husband, but she now wanted to move to Weaverville to be near her daughter. I suspected she wanted an agreement allowing sale of their one-level "highly marketable" (in her words) ranch home in Ohio as contingency (condition) to the purchase of our home.

I say "guessed," in that we never moved beyond initial discussions. Why? I wasn't really up for a move; I'd just had a minor surgical procedure; the woman mandated I respond to her offer by noon the next day. She said she was flying back to Ohio, but she was going to put an offer on some property before she left. She wanted it to be mine, but if we couldn't agree, she'd go with the other.

I told her if she needed an immediate answer, we'd have to pass. To tell the truth, I wasn't interested in selling to anyone who had the sale of their home as contingency. As realtors know, that situation is just too "iffy." The other home can languish; it's almost never as "highly marketable" as the owner thinks; I could never know the eccentricities of the market on the other end.

Following this, I promptly removed our "For Sale" sign. It was just as well: Our next-door neighbors and good friends had decided to sell their unit. Realizing a side-by-side sale was simply not in either of our best interests, we determined to wait another year.

Our neighbor sold their similarly designed unit, for $266,000, resulting in a net to them, of $250,000, after the pay-out of a 6% realtor commission.

We Sell

The following year, when we went back to Weaverville, in January, the selling market was ideal: Hamburg Crossing had no townhomes "For Sale." Sure, it was another bleak weather period but there's nothing like being the only contender for a prize... especially in a hotly-sought-after community, as is the case with Hamburg Crossing.

On Zillow, I posted our home for sale, with twenty-three pictures. I wrote up our listing in terms most favorable, capitalizing on all the extras I know the public wants: granite counters, maple cabinetry, engineered hardwoods (allows for sanding one time). I pointed out subtler aspects: a second floor that is completely private (not open loft as are other Villa II models), one that has its own heating and cooling control, the arguably best view in the complex, a Southern exposure that insures it's sunny. I made sure to mention our location off the central circular loop, which affords more privacy, a location apart from berms or retaining walls.

In short, I sold its virtues. To those who might want the one floor Canterbury unit, I offered that the Canterbury had been our initial preference, but we grew to love the Villa II, for it gave us, as a couple, our own space, since it had internal hallways connecting to other rooms and a second floor (where I worked as a writer). The rooms of a Canterbury model spin out from the center, like the spokes of a wheel, and as a result, real privacy is at a premium. I also mentioned the second floor master bedroom/bath suite is ideal for families visiting, offering: "Throw a mini-fridge in there and you need never see them, after a day of sight-seeing."

That statement often brought forth chuckles.

As to my own creation on the second floor, my brave (if crazy) attempt at free-hand painting a mural of trees on the slanted wall across from where we positioned the bed? I shared that I had painted this so our little three- month-old grandson could gaze up, into the trees, as we tended to him on the changing table. Everyone loved it and none of the eventual twelve people who came to see our unit had anything but raves for my efforts (so much for my saying "Leave the accessorizing to new buyers").

In all, we received three offers for our property. Two of the potential buyers were not represented by realtors. We went with the buyer who proposed cash purchase (financing for condo or townhome can be more difficult due to risk factors involved with plurality of ownership) and terms we could live with.

But it wasn't clear sailing from the git-go. A new realtor almost torpedoed the entire transaction before it was safely out of the gate (on the Zillow site, we offered a legitimate buyer broker commission of 2.5%).

Let me back up to explain: On a Friday night, at 6:00 P.M., I got an email request through Zillow from a buyer to see our unit. Our property had been advertised only a week. These potential buyers had seen my photos (with close-ups of the hardwood floors and granite counters, since those are vitally important to buyers)...the laundry room... the double garage with entrance into the house (important for security reasons). I included pictures of our view of nearby mountains and pastoral hillsides from the patio and the second floor. I even included a picture of the across- the-street farm to provide context of setting, as well as a shot of the margue-rite daisies that grace our place in the summer (ones we never enjoyed, since we were never there in the growing season).

I responded to the interested party via the number she pro-vided, but when I called, I got the recorder and left them a mes-sage. I didn't hear back until Sunday at 1:00 P.M., when Paul and I were in Hendersonville, about thirty-five miles away, having lunch. The woman asked: "Could we see your townhome today?" Since it was glorious weather, we hurried back to accommodate them, for a 4:00 P.M. showing.

They arrived, swept through, and were visibly impressed. They told me they'd been looking for a while. I asked the wife: "Are you working with a realtor?" (as a realtor, I know to ask this). She an-swered: "Uh...no...do I need one?" I answered: "No, we can do this together, and it will save both of us money. We can work out the terms (I mentioned I was a realtor in Rhode Island)...You'd prob-ably want inspections...We'd each have our own lawyers to make sure everything's done properly."

They left, saying they'd be in touch.

In the next couple of days, she asked me to provide them with our utility bills so they knew projected costs. Following my compil-ing and sending those, she told me—in an email—that they were "very interested.'" She said: "We're doing our homework in the next few days (a lighthearted reference to the fact we're both teach-ers): please be patient but know we really like your townhome."

Tuesday night I showed our unit to a couple from Hilton Head who were accompanied by their Keller Williams realtor. Joe and Buffy were disenchanted Hilton Head residents who shared with us that they'd grown tired of the heat...the traffic...the bugs. They now sought a mountain home. The man offered: "Your place is beauti-fully decorated," and Buffy asked, "Would you sell it furnished?"

I told her I'd like to comply, but we'd be taking most furnishings with us. Still, I was heartened by the fact imminent sale seemed probable.

On this perfect evening, they lingered on our patio, gazing dreamily at the mountains which were a hazy plum color in the distance. But I'd discover two hours later: They'd put an offer on another townhome, in Hendersonville.

On Wednesday, I got a call from a realtor with Coldwell Banker, one of the companies I'd worked for, in Rhode Island. Her buyers wanted a Friday appointment, at 11:00 A.M. I said "Sure, that'll work." This was my second realtor calling for a showing.

On Thursday, that same realtor called to say: "Oh, I should add that you've met my clients, already." I said: "Really...who are they?" She said their names. I was shocked. They were the same couple with whom I'd had the back and forth engagement several times... the same couple who'd come to me via Zillow ...the same who'd told me they weren't working with a realtor.

And because I'm a realtor, I knew immediately what had transpired. Somehow...somewhere...this realtor had suggested to our buyer: "Look, you can have a realtor's professional advice and you don't even have to pay for it (that's the case in most instances, for the usual listing commission of 6% is split between buying and selling broker, so the seller, in effect, pays the buyer broker commission, coming out of the proceeds at the closing). Buyers jump at this. Why wouldn't they?

But as realtor, here's what else I knew: This agent was decidedly not the "procuring cause" –the one who introduced the property in some form to the buyer (emails...drive-by's.. appointments) or one who was working with them, when we met (remember...I asked).

The buyer had found the property on Zillow, stated to me at our initial showing that she was not working with a realtor, and continued interacting with me on several occasions. I made the determination: I would not recognize this realtor, as a buyer broker, coming in at the eleventh hour (one who'd get $7,000, if I did recognize).

But I didn't tell the realtor that...yet.

Instead, I told her that I'd see them all on Friday. In preparation of the appointment, I typed up an explanation of why I wouldn't be paying this realtor a commission. Why did I do so? The public never truly understands how a realtor gets paid; this realtor wasn't procuring cause—I was. I wanted no confusion.

On that Friday, after a polite greeting at the door, I handed both buyer and realtor my typed explanation. They both seemed perplexed. I added: "I need to explain that I'll not be paying a buyer broker fee, in this instance, since (realtor whose name is withheld) isn't the procuring cause. The buyer and I have had several interactions before this realtor came on the scene."

Then, I looked directly at the buyer and said: "Of course, as buyer, you are free to use any realtor's services, but any commission for the realtor will not be coming out of our sales proceeds."

A pall descended, as both women tried to digest this. I knew I risked the buyer walking out, but I was also annoyed: I'd done far too much work to have a last-minute realtor swoop in, expecting a commission on this transaction.

When they went upstairs, there ensued a lengthy hushed conversation. Following that, the realtor was on her cell with her managing broker, doubtless asking "What should I do?" or "Can she (the seller) do this?"

When the buyer and realtor continued their talk on my driveway, I signaled that Paul and I had to leave for an appointment.

Later that day the realtor called to tell me she'd be coming over, with an offer.

When she arrived, she said she was now acting merely as "friend," no longer in buyer broker capacity. She knew the buyer, personally, for they were all tenants in the same apartment building. I had always suspected she'd offered her realtor services after the buyer told her their intention to purchase.

I asked her if a preapproval letter from financial institution accompanied the offer (standard practice), and unbelievably, she answered: "Oh, they're paying cash," as if that fact obviated need for proof. I told her the buyers would need a pre-approval letter, all the more, if they proposed a cash transaction.

I also told her: "Today, I took issue with your calling me 'honey.'" She countered with "Oh, that's just a Southern thing...I wasn't being rude." I said: "No, you didn't say it as casual Southern. When I said you didn't initiate buyer/seller relationship, here, you shot back with 'Look, honey, I've been working with (buyer name) for some time.'"

I added: "In the future, don't call me honey." Next, I added: "You know, I want to like you..." At that, she waved me off, saying, "Oh, it's not necessary for you to like me." I countered with: "'Not necessary?' Your friend wants my house...Yes, you very much want me to like you."

When she left, I read the offer: The buyers had come in low and in "additional provisions" section, of the offer, the realtor had written "included in this sale is the queen-sized cherry Restoration Hardware bed from second floor master suite (a $3,000 value)."

I fumed, inwardly. It was bad enough the offer was woefully short. It came with a provision we throw in our expensive bed, upstairs. (Personal property is never written into a real estate offer.)

The realtor emailed me the preapproval form the next day, but I sent notice that we wouldn't give a counter price. I feared more problems due to inept handling by an inexperienced realtor who'd given terrible advice to the buyers.

The following Sunday, we held an Open House where we met several new folks looking at Weaverville as their retirement home. As they they Ooohhed and Aaaahed throughout our townhome, I got a call. It was the buyer. She began haltingly...even apologized... said we could get beyond the difficult start. I listened. Real estate had taught me always to keep my eyes on the end-result. She was our potential buyer and we wanted to sell. Besides, as I said: I didn't blame her. I knew how the realtor had talked up the wisdom of having her represent them.

We agreed to start fresh. She told me their top offer and I accepted. It would be a sale between principals (buyer and seller) with no realtor fees, just as I planned initially. They'd meet with their lawyer to draw up a contract based on our mutually-agreed-upon terms regarding due diligence, earnest money, closing date; they'd have inspections within that due diligence period of two weeks.

In two days, I got the contract which we signed. At inspections, we left them and the inspector in our home, for three hours. The inspector told them ours was the best-maintained home he'd seen in his eight years of doing that business. I expected such. We'd had no problems. The one item that was found faulty was a leak in the coupling right under the kitchen sink. We hired a plumber to fix it and left paperwork attesting to such for the buyer (in case there were any future problems). The cost? $75.00.

We'd done the self-sale of our townhome in record time, but it was our Zillow listing, with pictures and verbiage, along with my considerable realtor skill, that helped to sell it. As back-up security, I paid a one-time fee of $299 to a friend who charged for "listing only" to get our townhome on statewide multiple listing (so realtors would see), but we never needed that, for our townhome sold immediately to that buyer we got through Zillow.

Our townhome sold for \$280,000, without the usual 6% realtor commission, meaning: To net \$280,000, with a realtor representing, we would've needed to sell at \$296,800. Selling for \$280,000 without a realtor's fee was good business for both the buyer and us.

To what do I ascribe success? As a professional realtor, I knew how to maximize our unit's potential, and frankly, our home was in great shape, with all the extras buyers want.

Below is the letter I gave to the buyer and realtor who accompanied buyer. Recall that I gave no advance notice on the phone to the realtor of my displeasure with the fact she now acted as Buyer Broker, when she requested the showing; in other words, I never said: "Oh, that's the couple I've been working with on several occasions, already." No, I knew to keep the goal in mind—the sale of the home (ours in this case)—a cardinal rule a realtor always learns.

Dear _____ *(A.K.A. as "Buyer"):*

I have determined to write this letter in that the public never fully understands how realtors are paid and I want no confusion. First off, my husband and I are pleased that you have such interest in our property since we love our townhome and have enjoyed living here for nine years.

But we need to make clear that we will not be paying this realtor a buyer broker fee.

When you first came to our home, it was through my Zillow listing with twenty-three photos. We agreed to show you our property. At that time, I asked if you were working with a realtor and you said "No—Do I need one?" I told you that having a realtor is not necessary...in fact, if we did this alone, we could save each other considerable money. I also told you that I am a realtor in Rhode Island (not licensed in NC) and added that we could both have our lawyers review the contract and as buyers, you can have inspections in the two-week period set aside for that purpose.

We then interacted several times after this, with you asking me to present our utility bills so you could determine if all was in your price range. I did so and I answered all your other questions regarding the community, etc.

Now, today, you have arrived with a realtor who is presumably acting in buyer broker capacity. Having this individual advise you is your choice, of course, but we do need to make clear that her commission will not be coming out of our sellers' side of the transaction (as it often does in most real estate sales,) since we are the "procuring cause" in this instance, meaning we are the sellers with whom you interacted on all previous occasions of visit, emails, etc.

Of course, you are free to use your realtor but her commission will need to come from you.
Most sincerely,
Colleen Kelly and Paul Gates

P. S. One reason I could be so successful in the self-sale of our townhome is my considerable training as professional realtor. Most of the public rightly see "For Sale by Owner" (pronounced FIS-BO in the vernacular) as an area fraught with problems, regarding what is for most folks their biggest, single, lifetime purchase or sale. They are fearful regarding how they should proceed, don't understand disclosures (what the owner must disclose regarding his property), are not privy to the time constraints contracts delineate, do not understand rights and obligations of both sellers and buyers.

For instance, once the Purchase & Sale contract is signed, inspections follow and often negotiations accompany, meaning a fine dance ensues to bring all parties to closure.

The single most problematic aspect in self-sale is the fact the owner/seller is emotionally-tied to his property and does not view its sale as business transaction. That problem is mitigated when an objective party—a real estate professional—represents the seller.

Photo below is of our home and the upstairs suite with the trees I painted on the ceiling.

What We Did with the Furniture

When we went under contract with the buyers, I knew I had to go into high gear, selling furniture we wouldn't bring back to Rhode Island and making arrangements to transport those we would.

This would be a daunting task since our residence was close to 2000 square feet, fully-furnished.

With furniture sale in mind, we visited consignment stores in the region that I thought would have the best shot at getting us good prices. I wanted only those that had been in business for some time, those that had good reputations, those in high traffic areas.

When we began our North Carolina experience, we bought all new furniture for our townhome. After nine years, it was all in excellent condition, for we are two adults who don't smoke; we have no pets and no children living with us. In addition, we'd had relatively few visitors over the course of our years in North Carolina.

So, our townhome and furnishings retained an almost-new appearance. I know that because of the positive reaction of people who came to our Open Houses. Then, too, there was that husband who said our home was "beautifully furnished," while his wife asked "could we sell it furnished?"

The consignment shop owners I interviewed came to our home to assess the items, and I decided to hire Frugal Décor, a business in Asheville that sits at the top of a hill, one of the many we visited when we moved to Asheville. I chose them because they sold high-end furnishings of good quality, and their layout was large and well-designed, showcasing furnishings artistically, in their best light. The goods weren't merely warehoused.

Next, I took photos of all the furnishings we'd sell, thus enabling me to recall better what I had entrusted them with. This was a far better plan than a mere listing of items, and on the appointed day, their men arrived to pack up and take a truckload of items.

The movers were careful; they had the requisite blanket wraps for fragile items; they knew what they were doing (remember—Paul could evaluate their work since he is a household mover by profession).

Now, what remained for me to do was arrange the person who'd transport our other furnishings to Rhode Island. I had already determined the expensive Ethan Allen console and china closet would go to Rhode Island with us, and our North Carolina couch would replace our 20-year-old one in our Rhode Island living room.

I sold some items on Craigslist, such as the twin daybed, with its comforter and pillows. A young woman answering my ad bought it, dismantled it, and strapped it onto her SUV. We were impressed.

Another woman bought two child Adirondack rockers, with Moose pillows for her little ones. They, too, were perfect and never got the wear I'd hoped they would from our grandchildren.

By the time all was said and done, we had enough remaining furniture to fill a straight truck.

Our mover was a man I met in a line at the Steak 'n Shake, in Weaverville, a serendipitous event that makes me believe meeting him was meant to be, for that occasion was the one and only time we had been to that fast food restaurant.

I told him Paul and I were there, taking a break from packing up our household. He said he moved furniture for folks who were going to different states, and I happily took his business card. He came to our home the following week and appraised the job. We hired him and set a date for the move. He had excellent references. In fact, he'd moved our next-door neighbor the spring before, when they took their furnishings to Florida, a fact even he didn't realize until he came to our home.

In the meantime, we collected boxes and began the arduous task of packing up everything. In the time ahead, we spent a few hours each day, doing this. I regretted the many pictures we'd hung on our neutral walls, since taking them down left holes, and I feared wall damage might become an issue at the walk-thru. (i.e. A buyer of a house I sold in Rhode Island insisted on—and got– $2,000 for painting when he noted the condition of walls, once the pictures were taken down.)

So, I painted, taking paint chips to Ace hardware, in Weaverville, and getting new paint matched, as closely as possible. Word of caution here: It's almost impossible to really match paint, even with their high-tech machinery that supposedly produces the same color as the ten-year-old paint on one's walls.

Result? I often had to repaint an entire wall, since the brush strokes over one section always showed discrepancy. A friend suggested a brilliant solution as I neared the end of my painting: Make a paste of Spackle (or some similar fill) and mix it with the new paint and carefully fill in those holes. When I did this, I reduced my redo efforts considerably.

If I were ever to go into a new residence again, I might just keep the walls bare and showcase art on easels.

A year after our return to Rhode Island, many furnishings we brought still sat in our garage, since in the interim we had had new hardwoods installed in our Rhode Island home. Following that installation, we made decisions, regarding what to sell.

Then we hired a Rhode Island consignment group, Estate Sales, in West Warwick, to sell items we definitely didn't want.

In both instances, we realized far more by selling unwanted furnishings through these vendors than we would have, if we had gone the route of yard sales or Craigslist.

The good news? If we ever need to move again, it should be easy. Our home is sparsely furnished now; I don't hang pictures on recently painted walls. The heaviest work is done, and the clutter is gone.

As we get older, we want fewer items. We're de-cluttering our lives, but I find it ironic that the purchase and sale of our North Carolina home spurred on final decision-making regarding our Rhode Island home, as well.

Legal Mayhem

I f I've learned anything in the legal realm, from our recent real estate transaction, it is: Ask, specifically, what a lawyer will do for you, as your representative in home sale, when you hire his or her services. Ask, too, what won't be included.

In the weeks following the signing of the contract, we knew we needed a legal stand-in for the closing, since we wouldn't still be in Asheville, by the closing. Paul and I had committed to a *Grandpa and the Truck* show in front of a big elementary school audience, back in Rhode Island. With that in mind, we hired a lawyer, one a friend recommended.

In full disclosure mode, I admit: I never asked for a specific delineation of what the lawyer would do for us in this transaction, and she never specified. I assumed the transaction would go as I'd witnessed in countless real estate closings, during my years as professional realtor in Rhode Island.

I'd chosen a lawyer a friend referred, but I'd learn, shortly into her firm's representation that she'd passed us on to another lawyer in her firm. That lawyer informed us we'd be mostly interacting with her legal assistant.

I feared a muddied chain of command and the potential for "things forgotten," but I accepted the situation.

Somewhere, during the days leading up to the closing, I had asked, in an email, of my attorney, what I should do about house keys. I had arranged with a friend to open our townhome the day before closing to allow buyers a walk-through, on Monday, May 18, but I told my friend not to give the keys to the buyers, at that time.

Having gotten no response regarding the keys, I followed protocol for real estate transactions in Rhode Island, meaning I had my friend deliver keys to the buyer's attorney just before the closing that was scheduled for 11:00 A.M., on Tuesday, the 19th of May.

To facilitate immediate wiring of funds into our account, we'd given the legal assistant our bank's routing number and our checking account number. We had every reason to expect the recording of the deed would happen the same day (usual procedure) as the closing, especially since the closing was scheduled in the morning.

Only that didn't happen.

I kept checking on the afternoon of the 19th for confirmation the funds had been deposited in our account, but nothing showed up. I called the office for deed recording and they said there'd been no recording. I was advised by my attorney's office to be patient. Recording would most likely happen the next morning.

But my concern was: If the deed hadn't yet been recorded and keys had been turned over to the buyers, at closing, Paul and I were legally liable for any problems that might occur at the townhome.

When I called my lawyer about my concern, she said: "If the keys were turned over, before the deed is recorded, you'll have to get your friend to go back and get those keys from the lawyer."

She followed that up with: "Our office never gives keys until after the actual recording's been done."

I replied: "But I had asked your office about this very situation days ago. It's not possible for us to retrieve the keys! The closing was six hours ago." Next, I was treated to the one-liner I'd hear often, from this lawyer who was also the head of the firm: "We don't handle that."

To be clear: All I'd done in that earlier email was ask what needed to be done, regarding the keys; I never asked the law firm to handle them.

I was apoplectic. In my opinion, she side-stepped responsibility for ignoring my question. Then, too, she never apologized for the missed communication.

All night I sweated out the reality we were liable for any problems. It wasn't groundless fear, for the husband of the buyer couple had serious recent health problems. I knew an accident in the property we still officially owned would mean we were liable.

The next morning, I began calling and emailing my lawyer with a CC to the legal assistant and the head lawyer. The assistant told me at 10:00 A.M.: "The buyer's attorney has recorded the deed. You're all set. If your money doesn't appear in a couple of hours, let me know." She added that that buyer attorney said he hadn't given the keys to the buyer, at closing (he had).

By 2:00 P.M., when I still didn't see the money in our account, I called the Deeds office. The buyer's attorney had not been in. (They knew him and his staff.) The buyers' attorney had misrepresented a key fact to my lawyer's legal assistant.

In the meantime, the buyer called. She just wanted me to know how thrilled she was with everything. I told her things weren't as smooth on our end, that we'd still not gotten the money (now, over twenty-four hours later). I asked what time, the day before, the signing took place. She told me their lawyer was an hour late for the closing; they'd signed all documents at 12:00 noon; and that their lawyer had given her the keys at that time. So, his telling me he'd never turned over the keys to buyers was lie #2 for this lawyer.

I called our own legal assistant to insist the head lawyer make the call to the buyer's attorney's office, demanding recording and wiring of our money.

At 3:30 P.M. the day after the closing, the buyer's attorney finally recorded.

I emailed the buyer's attorney, requesting a copy of the HUD sheet, while I awaited the hard copy.

I sent an email summation to our lawyer as to why I was disgusted with what happened, regarding her law firm's representation. Throughout the process, I checked with a former realtor who lived in our complex to make sure I wasn't out of line in my expectations of our lawyer. He was stunned at the poor service we received.

The response? Basically, our lawyer suggested our self-sale was the problem: If we'd gone the usual route of seller represented by a realtor (remember, I was a professional realtor, in R.I.), I'd have avoided these issues.

By Thursday, two days after closing, I still hadn't received an e-mail copy of the HUD sheet (contract signed by all parties), prompting a final call to my lawyer. The response? The head lawyer said: "We don't involve ourselves in that aspect. You'll have to contact the buyer's attorney. He initiates documents."

So, my question remains: What did our lawyer do for her fee? Had I hired her to merely sign documents whose terms the buyer and I created, documents initiated by the buyers' attorney?

My ignorance of the lines of responsibility and my lawyers' failure to communicate those same became critical when I was confronted with an inept and irresponsible buyer lawyer, one who obviously only operated on a schedule convenient to him.

I'll say this, too: In this nerve-wracking interaction, I felt alone. I felt my own lawyers hung me out to dry.

In the future, I'll clearly delineate the role of each professional whose services I seek and I'd make certain (even IF I utilize a realtor as selling broker) keys are never turned over until after the deed is recorded, since I'm still official owner and liable for any problems before that recording.

Furthermore, since it was the buyers' lawyer that caused all the initial delays, if house keys weren't to be turned over until after the recording, that reality would have automatically spurred him the buyer attorney to record as soon as possible or face an angry client (his own).

As an aside, a year later I still haven't gotten a hard copy (paper version) of the sales agreement (HUD).

Why We Left Asheville

This is the topic everyone wants to know about.

In my guest-speaking, folks always ask: "Why did you leave Asheville? What brought you back to Rhode Island?"

I will say this: We enjoyed most of our nine years in Asheville, except, understandably, the timeframe immediately following the accident. To this day, I have many friends in Asheville and in retrospect, I am grateful for our years in that beautiful region.

But, in the end, we returned to the land of my roots. I say 'my' because Paul was born and raised in Arkansas. It's just that he re-raised himself as Rhode Islander over the next fifty-plus years.

Oversight of both properties had become cumbersome, especially since tough winters affect the northern one. We worried, constantly, over the years, about that home's weathering of storms and designated a person back home who made regular home wellness checks, but we were aware that a monster problem (like a water pipe break) could wreak havoc before it was even detected.

After the accident, juggling two homes became increasingly difficult, for I took on more of the day-to-day operations, for both places. So, our choice: Did we really want to live in Asheville, solely, for the rest of our lives? It would mean leaving the Northeast... leaving Rhode Island, a tiny state we both loved, for its natural beauty...its navigable qualities (forty-five minutes from north to south)...its quaint and diverse villages...its history...its proximity to New York and Boston...its ocean frontage...its unabashed charm?

On a scale of 1 to 10 (10 being highest), I'd always clocked Rhode Island's "Cuteness Factor" as a 9.

I'd always considered that many who preferred Asheville's beauty came from regions that couldn't measure up, for they appeared to believe the mountains far surpassed any of their own home state's virtues.

Maybe winter's extreme cold in their former state was the deciding factor.

As I got older, I considered, too: "We're not going to be hiking about those mountains, in our 80's." Because I have MS, I have a tough time doing that even now. And we couldn't bike in Asheville, frequently limited as we were to the Biltmore House grounds for this activity. There were no miles-long, designated bike paths set aside for those of us who love that activity. In Asheville, we'd need to "Share the road" with automobiles—something with which we're never comfortable. I'd miss the long, dedicated bike trails in Rhode Island, where we ride along the ocean or former railroad trails that pass historic mills.

In the end, the biggest factor in swaying us to move back home was "familiarity."

I knew I'd miss the way the sun rises above the tall hemlock trees on our Rhode Island property; the local, many-acre park, where we go for walks; the harbor just below our hillside home, where all manner of boats bob; the old, moss-covered stone walls that meander through our neighborhood, the marbled headstone markers in the historic cemetery that signify neighbors of an earlier era.

And in another strange recognition, I missed all the natural ponds, lakes and waterways, besides the ocean, that Rhode Island enjoys. I didn't find these in western North Carolina where if water presents, it's often a shallow stream or occasional man-made, too-perfectly-round lake. I found that reality troubling for a girl who's grown up with natural waterways all around.

I'd miss nearby shops where we know the merchants...the restaurant staff of eateries who know our every culinary preference and greet us by name when we enter.

I'd miss the quaint and colorful villages of Chepachet, Little Compton, Wickford, and others that are all so close to each other, each having its own distinct personality. Yes, being from such a small state, I love the short distances we travel to enter those totally different worlds.

I love the vistas around every corner...the sea grass...the marshes.

I'd miss the pounding surf.

In my decision-making, I thought of my mother. At the end of her life, she had her choice: "Did she want to go to Maine (where another sibling and a nursing home awaited) or did she wish to remain in Rhode Island?"

Her reply was swift and loud: "Hell...no...I'm not going to Maine."

Frankly, she never liked the seemingly vast distances between homes on our many trips to that region to visit my sister. We Rhode Islanders get adjusted to short distances, going anywhere.

My mother was a simple woman who was the quintessential 1950's homemaker. She lived for Fridays, her one day of the week, when she dropped my father off at school (he was principal) and got to have the family car to run household errands. She enjoyed her day, immensely, as she first visited her Cranston hairdresser for the weekly ritual, whereby Enzo washed, dried, and pinned up her hair into her trademark French twist. Following that, she went shopping at the Mall, stopped at the liquor store, for the week's supply of wine, made a quick run to the cleaners, and followed all up with grocery shopping.

All before the 3:00 o'clock return of us kids from school.

This was her schedule for many, many years.

That schedule, with its familiarity of roads, shops, and stops grounded her. At 90, she didn't want to have to process a whole new region, and I fully recognized that, when memory wanes (as it does at advanced age), one seeks familiar prompts all the more.

It's no time to accommodate to a whole new set of stimuli, unless one has been doing that her entire life (in which case, she has no real grounding).

Because I saw her reaction to a proposed new environment, at her advanced age, I considered what I'd face, if I made my permanent, final home in Asheville.

In the end, my mother went to a nursing home where her mother had gone, before her, a place I'll doubtless go, too. Often, upon visiting, I'd bring her out, in her wheelchair, on oceanside walks along the cliffs, when she breathed deep the salt air. She'd say: "I always wanted to live by the sea."

I'd bring her on rides where she'd revisit her childhood. She'd point out where her family's old home had been, alongside the river, where her brothers would tempt fate and cross the slippery dam.

Often, in the summer, we'd stop for a root beer float at her favorite vendor, Newport Creamery, or get an iced coffee. Such memory-rekindling would have been unavailable to her in Maine.

My mother always knew something I didn't–familiarity comforts mightily, especially when one is old.

In the end, it might be one of the few things that truly matter.

One Year Out from Sale

We began assessing our full year residence back home in Rhode Island a year after the sale of our townhome. The weather that winter was stunningly mild, as opposed to the thirty-six inches of snow that fell –and stayed–the winter before.

We feared we'd be readjusting to that reality.

Before the fiercest part of winter, we planned to check on rental units in Florida, where other friends stayed for two to three months, but we did not. The impetus for going was removed by the fact the weather was co-operating and we were just tired.

Then there was the fact that in Rhode Island I'm published, as a regular Op-Ed columnist in the *Providence Journal*, and my columns began running in my hometown newspaper, the *Kent County Daily Times*, as well.

I guest-speak, too, a role that has grown as a result of my columns.

Paul has lost cognitive ability. His memory has been tracked since that first year following the accident, and he's now part of a double blind study for a new memory drug, for Alzheimer's, but neither his doctor nor we know if he gets the medicine or if he gets a placebo (hence the term "double blind"). Doctors had warned us the anoxic period, after he choked, might spur on a decline in mental functioning. We do the best we can under the circumstances.

I know one thing: He is far happier here in Rhode Island. He has his beloved yard; he has his workman's garage (where all his tools are).

We go biking on the many trails, an activity we both love.

I'm happier, too, knowing he's happy.

This book is my first official step into publishing a book for adults. Oh, I produced *Grandpa and the Truck* children's books (1 and 2) but they were based on Paul's thirty years on the road as a long-haul trucker, delivering household furnishings all over the country. I have six to eight more of these children's books in the wings, to be published in future.

This book tracks my view of things as a couple who left their home state for a new beginning in their retirement town, what they found, and why they ultimately left.

I look back on our Asheville experience with the belief that it was important. It helped me find my place and hone my writer's voice. Maybe I had to go away to do that.

The upper level of our townhome became my writer's domain. I'd look over the beautiful mountains and find solace in their immutability. Then, I'd go back to my writing, refreshed.

I am forever struck by the twin irony of two disastrous events that shaped me, in Asheville.

The gentler environment we sought–the less frenzied corridor of life, away from the Northeast– became the thing that almost did us in, for on an infrequently traveled mountain road, Paul suffered the accident. That event colored all else.

Then, too, a short while after we left, a member of my women's group, Tina Kessinger, was murdered in Asheville.

The following is an account I wrote in her honor.

And One of Us Was Murdered

In the United States, a person is murdered every two hours. Mostly, that occurs in cities. According to the latest Federal Bureau of Investigation figures of crime in the United States (2014), 'There were an estimated 1,165,383 violent crimes (murder and non-negligent homicides, rapes, robberies, and aggravated assaults) reported by law enforcement.' Four hundred and eight-nine of those happened in North Carolina.

My friend was a recent victim of a highly published violent crime, occurring in Asheville, North Carolina.

Christina (Tina) Kessinger, a member of our afore-mentioned women's group, was murdered in Asheville on February 12, 2016. Her name will be included in all national violent crime statistics from 2016 on.

Pretty and petite, Tina stood at 5' 2," probably posing no threat to a criminal who would suppose she could not put up much of a fight. She was a gentle soul, known in our group for baking beautiful cakes for friends' birthdays, bringing them to whatever restaurant we women favored for our celebration.

She'd become a realtor in recent years and asked my advice regarding that profession, since I'd been a realtor, following my three decade teaching career, in Rhode Island. I gave her tips on how to pass the exam and also accompanied her to Asheville business meet-up's, thinking to help her crack into a field which tends to be more challenging, if one enters later in life. I knew the hurdles she'd face.

Tina and I also shared a career as writer, with both of us freelancing for various publications. In addition, we both wrote blogs. She wrote a column about Paul and me for her "Over 50 in Asheville" blog, since she found our story regarding how we began publishing our children's books, *Grandpa and the Truck* compelling and inspiring.

Tina, herself, had come to Asheville from Arizona, where she'd lived for many years, working as a clerk in a real estate company. She was an activist, too, not unlike many who come to this region, similarly concerned for the earth and its future, taking on projects to insure environmental beauty and sustainability. She committed to improving a garden across from the Asheville Civic Center and spearheaded a successful project to get a traffic light installed at a crosswalk in her neighborhood, where a pedestrian was killed the year before, as she crossed the street.

Tina succeeded in whatever she put her mind to.

An avowed animal lover, she worked tirelessly to bring awareness in that quarter, often posting pictures of animals available for adoption.

For all these reasons, we, her friends, were shocked with what happened to her, for she was a fearless advocate of all who needed support and protection. In the end, she became a victim.

It was a Friday afternoon, around 3:30 P.M., when Tina went for a few things at the market. When she walked back to her car, she was accosted by a man, wielding a screwdriver. He ordered her to go with him to her car.

Presumably directing her to a mostly vacant office building around the corner, he had her park the car, get out, and there he attacked her, plunging the screwdriver into her. He then picked her up and put her in the dumpster, where she was later found by a cleaning crew discarding products they'd used in that building. One of them heard her moans and noted blood on the lid when he opened it.

Not wishing to disturb the crime scene, one worker climbed into the bin to stay with Tina, while the other went to call police. Medics revived Tina at the scene, but she died later, at the hospital.

Following the alleged assault on Tina, the assailant, James Michael Norton, 29, took Tina's car to Marshall, to a relative's house, where he stayed the night.

An alert neighbor called police about the car parked in front of the mother's house, a car the neighbor had seen on the news.

When police searched Tina's 2010 Toyota Corolla, Norton came out of the house and when police asked him why he had the car, he said it "was his girlfriend's" and he "was using it because his had broken down." In the follow-up search of the relative's home, police found the screwdriver and some of Tina's belongings. At that, Norton was taken into custody.

Norton had been released from prison one year before, on February 15, 2015, following his larceny of a motor vehicle and altering a serial number, after serving a sentence of at least ten months. In 2013, he'd attacked a Mission hospital worker with a sharpened stake.

His criminal history is peppered with felony convictions across several counties, including larceny over $1,000 and credit card theft in Buncombe County, breaking and entering in Madison County, and drug possession in Henderson County, according to Department of Corrections' records.

As of this date, Norton is deemed incompetent to stand trial, yet he remains charged with first degree murder and robbery with a dangerous weapon.

Both Paul's almost death on a back road in Weaverville and our friend's murder brought us all the realization that, at any time, one can meet up with darker forces.

What happened to our dear friend Tina Kessinger will ever be a stark reminder that evil lurks everywhere—even in Asheville. Her picture is below.

Part II: We Adjust to Our New Region

How We Chose Our Retirement State

Just one of the many natural visual displays in western North Carolina. These falls are outside the town of Highlands.

Many ask us: "Why the Tarheel state of North Carolina?" Ours was a studied approach. We spent approximately ten years searching and researching the entire Eastern coast from Maine to Key West, in our quest to find our retirement state, with me pretty much thinking: "It's never going to happen...I'll not find a place where I feel comfortable enough to put down roots."

At 61 years of age, I'd never lived outside of Rhode Island, that tiny splotch on the Northeast coast that bears the moniker "The Ocean State," that smallest state of our great nation, the land of clamcakes and "chowdah," a crazy accent as in "pahk the cah," a state bearing the moniker, Rogue Island, for its notoriety of shady characters who seek and keep public office. (See the book, *The Prince of Providence,* chronicling the life of the Mayor of that fair city, a felon revered by the masses.)

When one is a Rhode Islander, she gets used to getting anywhere fast. It's not like Pennsylvania or Virginia which take several hours to traverse.

In addition, Rhode Island population is wonderfully diverse due to the state's former glory as a commercial hub when the Industrial Revolution was at its peak. During that time, Providence, our state's capital city, was considered the nation's center for jewelry manufacturing. My own hometown, West Warwick, had, as its main commerce–fabric. Lace and cotton were two staples; Fruit of the Loom was born there. To fill factory jobs, waves of immigrants who lent their cultural customs, foods, beliefs arrived. Rhode Island became a true melting pot, welcoming ethnic groups from all over.

Today, most of the mills are vacant and some have been converted to loft condominiums. But our little state lags in commercial enterprise, despite the fact it offers pretty much everything else: gorgeous scenery; irrefutably fine dining, a refurbished downtown; great universities, Newport and Block Island, and those beaches, etc.

And if you can't find what you want in Rhode Island, New York City, Boston, and the mountains of upstate New York, New Hampshire, and Vermont are within easy driving range.

But living in Rhode Island poses dilemmas: mounting tax problems, as well as a climate that offers too harsh—and long–a winter, especially for older folks.

With that in mind, Paul and I searched up and down the coastline from Maine to Key West, hoping to discover where we'd like to live as alternative. We dismissed the gated, coastal communities we looked at, for the facts they enjoyed boating or golfing rights, and we are neither boaters nor golfers.

We visited most of the places touted as "Best Retirement Towns" but we kept dismissing each as too flat...too hot... too congested.

And because we feared floods, insurance costs (hurricanes), and maintenance problems with coastal properties, we went inland.

That's when we found, like Little Red Riding Hood, the one that was "just right."

Asheville, North Carolina, is a hamlet nestled in the Blue Ridge/ Smoky Mountains, seven hours inland from the coast. Some say the region's rife with a mystic pull due to its geographic location which may also help explain its mysterious pull—one that some define as an energy vortex.

Some even say: Like the Oracle at Delphi, in Greece, the mysterious pull allegedly affects some more than others, and that pull may act like an agent of attraction.

But I have to say, I wasn't smitten with Asheville, immediately.

Coming into downtown Asheville, my first impression was: "What's so great about this place?" Its commercial center seemed stuck in time, with art deco facades on buildings harkening back to the 1920's. It was quiet and unassuming, lacking the frenetic pace of other retirement areas we visited, a singular trait that ironically grew more appealing over the next several days.

The mountains charm; the sky glows fuchsia at dusk, the laid-back atmosphere soothes. Musicians abound and play outside various shops; an abundance of green grocers vie for one's business; massage therapists offer quick chair massages in those same markets; the health industry is alive and well. (After all, the purifying mountain air made Asheville a mecca for affluent Americans, treating their tuberculosis in the 1920's.)

The topography of winding hillside roads, edged with forests, was familiar to me. Asheville feels like the America I grew up in fifty years ago.

The University of North Carolina (Asheville campus) offers College for Seniors where the older set can take courses at much-lowered rates without the homework requirement (like auditing— one takes courses for simple enjoyment). We've sharpened our skills at some things and satisfied interest in others.

Paul and I moved into a townhome community in the sleepy community of Weaverville, almost ten miles north of downtown, a town whose main attractions for us included the New York City-style coffee shop, Well-Bred Café, and the unassuming Blue Mountain Pizza (where musicians jam on Wednesday nights).

While living in Weaverville, we hiked the mountains (they're called the "gentle mountains," for they're negotiable, as opposed to the sheer cliffs of the Rockies); we ate out a lot because it's far cheaper than dining out in New England; we volunteered services (I taught at the jail, while he ferried the blood supply to Charlotte for the Red Cross). Our townhome community was wonderful and supportive. People here become family, since almost everyone's from "away."

But throughout our nine years in Asheville, we kept another foot in Rhode Island. Was it counter-productive, tax-wise? Sure, for we paid both town and county taxes for our North Carolina home (there's a state income tax for residents that didn't apply to us since we were still primary residents of Rhode Island), and we paid a state income tax to Rhode Island, as well as city taxes for our home there.

But we couldn't seem to vacate the region where I grew up, one Paul's grown to love. There came a time, when we did have to make that final decision, since the financial burden was becoming unsustainable. After all, the plan was to ease into Southern living over time and slowly disconnect from New England, eventually living solely in western North Carolina.

For the years we alternated between North Carolina and Rhode Island, we considered we were helping keep those states' economies afloat. And we did without other things.

Was our living there for nine years a wise choice?

We think so, but the accident and its attending fall-out forced us to reassess all.

Western North Carolina mountains cast a smoky, blue-ish haze, hence the names Smoky and Blue Ridge Mountains readily apply.

First Overtures

Asheville is an artists' haven, a naturalists' mecca, a place where bungalows and multi-million dollar mansions intermingle, the latter often poised precipitously on mountainsides.

The downside of this juxtaposition from this former realtor's view? There's little to no zoning. So, it's entirely possible for trailers and trailer parks to pop up alongside $700,000 homes.

Our Wish List for our new home, in a more southern state, included the following: we wanted four distinct seasons, with none of them too extreme; good investment value (since we can't recoup financial loss at our age, the region had to demonstrate rising value, as opposed to flat or negative return); friendly community; manageable driving distance to Rhode Island; reasonable cost of living; good medical services; volunteer opportunities; and variety of outdoor activities.

In that search, we noted many of our peer group doing the same, in coffee shops, hunkered over real estate magazines, discussing the merits of gated communities, theme villages for boating, golfing, and shopping enthusiasts.

We recognized we were part of a growing national trend of active seniors in search of a home for the next phase of their lives.

Early in the process, we considered buying in St. Petersburg and Naples, Florida, but I dreaded what would be, for me, too-hot temperatures most of the year; Paul feared hurricanes, and attending rise in insurance costs, since many of the condominiums that had once been oceanside hotels were dangerously close to encroaching seas, with high tides lapping at their foundations. Friends of ours who did buy in coastal regions of Florida said they were shocked, following the wreckage of a hurricane, that despite the fact they were several rows back from front condos facing the ocean, the entire condominium community absorbed the cost of repair. Communal ownership means all bear the burden.

With that knowledge, we pushed on in our search.

Next, we swung inland and headed to Asheville, a western North Carolina town which has consistently headed or placed high on the above-mentioned lists.

Coming into Asheville, Interstate 40 winds along spectacular mountain passes and finally slices through a sheer rock corridor that spills into the downtown region. Asheville appears almost a bas relief against the backdrop of the Smokey, Blue Ridge, and Appalachian Mountains, one whose 1920's architecture and faded store marquees suggest a bygone era. Upon closer inspection, however, one notes Sushi shops, day spas and salons, coffee boutiques, art galleries, and restaurants that signal growth and prosperity. Asheville is a town on the move, one whose population has mushroomed in recent years, a town with a liberal political bent, an enclave of blue in a predominantly red state.

The commitment appears to be "Health first" with many businesses the brainchild of disenchanted types who traded the maniacal pace of the Northeast for this slower, more relaxed atmosphere. We met many 30 to 40 year old's, too, who said they "had to get out of that Northeast corridor."

It's really not unusual that we'd have chosen Asheville for perhaps something called to me, beyond the obvious.

As a realtor, I knew to follow a regimen I prescribe for buyers anywhere: tour the area by car, first, over a period of time, day and night, to get a feel for if the area will be right for you.

Once we knew Asheville was where we wanted to live, we sought a professional realtor to help us in that process, for I recognize it's risky enough, in one's home state, buying property without a realtor's help; it's lunacy to try this out-of-state. My top concern was avoiding a property near a landfill or Superfund site and I shared that with our realtor.

For, what seems pristine on the exterior may hide awful truths. Love Canal in Buffalo, New York, where Hooker Chemical polluted a significant part of a neighborhood, in the 1970's, taught all of my generation that lesson. Children playing on recreational fields during a dry spring found themselves ankle-deep in liquid toxins, a product of that company getting rid of its chemical waste into the surrounding community, destroying residents' health and home value. The only good to come out of this was the government's enacting a watchdog agency (Superfund.com) that identifies these sites and qualifies the nature of their hazards (more on that in later chapter).

But, it still falls to the buyer to do the research.

After several days, we selected a townhome community. Both the builder and we went back and forth in negotiations, where we insisted on what we wanted. Because our realtor worked for the company that was selling these condominiums, I mitigated any worries by asking specifics: "Is there anything that might adversely affect our investment value down the line? Specifically, were there any regional or neighborhood issues? Are there any landfills nearby?" "We wanted ALL information on units in that complex: "How much were they priced at (list price)?" "How much did they sell for?" "How long were they on market before sale?" We also wanted ALL the comparables of similar properties within a twenty-five mile radius. Armed with that information, we could determine fair market value and what we wished to offer. Negotiations went back and forth; we finally agreed on price and terms; and we went under contract.

On December 29, 2006, we made the trek, heavily laden with household furnishings in a truck driven by Paul while I followed behind in a loaded-down SUV. It took us sixteen hours to get from Rhode Island to North Carolina, and when we hit the last stretch, through the mountains, all I could see were the amber back lights of his pick-up truck, due to the thick, impenetrable fog. It occurred to me that if Paul headed wrong and went over the highway embankment, I'd no doubt follow. We had buttoned up everything back home, canceled mail and newspapers, put some utilities on hold, and initiated deliveries to our new home.

When we arrived for the walk-thru the day before closing (final check before taking possession), we noted wall-to-wall carpeting, counter to our agreement. Oh, it was good grade and attractive, but we had specified *no carpeting.* In addition, there was no refrigerator, although I listed all on the Purchase & Sale—*stove, refrigerator, and dishwasher* (important in that North Carolina sales include stove and dishwasher but strangely enough, exclude refrigerator; the buyer usually has to absorb that cost).

At the walk-thru, a Punch-List (items to be remedied) was developed and the builder's representative and we signed. Carpeting was removed by workmen the next day and the refrigerator was delivered. Over the next several weeks, the builder's contractors attended to all needs flagged on the Punch List. If they forgot, we reminded them and kept the list with items crossed off as each was completed (I obtained construction foreman's cell number at the walk-thru so we could access him as needed).

So, how did we do our first year? We discovered we were of the minority of folks who stayed through the winter, as many in our new community headed to Florida, after the holidays, with intention to return in the spring.

North Carolina had some cold days, but basically we enjoyed many sixty-degree days, allowing us to picnic outdoors, ride bikes, jog, walk, hike, etc. Because Asheville's population has exploded in recent years, assimilation is fairly easy with clubs and groups of every genre to facilitate newcomer adjustment.

That first year I volunteered at the Buncombe County Jail on Thursday evenings, teaching women English and writing skills. We enjoyed a wonderfully eclectic restaurant scene; we found the food markets excellent; and the crafts real art pieces. We visited small towns nestled in the mountain regions, each having its own personality.

On the downside, we expected furniture prices to be lower in the "Furniture Capital of the United States—Hickory, N.C." but in this, we were mistaken. We were told by one salesperson that most furniture is made in Asia and merely warehoused in Hickory, then shipped elsewhere in the United States. As a result, furniture there is no less expensive than elsewhere.

Our condominium association was comprised of a group committed to making a positive difference: the Capital Funds, Building, and Grounds Committees kept the builder and developer responsive to buyer agreements, while the Social Committee organized occasions for fun and social interaction. The clubhouse provided a central meeting area, grille, pool table, state-of-the-art exercise equipment and outdoor pool.

Financially, we never lost money on our investment, in the nine years since purchase, despite the housing market's tank shortly after we bought. But we never made money either. We've since learned that had we kept our townhome a year or two longer, we might have realized a nice profit since Asheville is booming—especially the region north of downtown where we lived.

In the end, it's all about the fit between the community and the newcomer. We just know that we felt comfortable in this western North Carolina town, from the outset, but it definitely helped that I knew how to navigate tricky real estate waters.

Was Our Choice of
Asheville Subliminal?

People who discover we live in Rhode Island most of the year always say: "Oh, I've been to Newport..." as if Newport defines Rhode Island. Well, Newport, a town on Aquidneck Island, off Rhode Island's main coastline, is a distinct entity whose reality defies the myth that "Folks are super-wealthy in this town."

In other words, most Newport residents are ordinary, working-class folks.

Newport's mega-mansions are a reflection of an earlier era, when the Carnegies, Rockefellers, and Vanderbilts, the supposed "Robber Barons of America" (who ironically don't look so bad right now, considering their contributions to museums, galleries, and libraries), built "summer cottages" along the Newport coastline that vie in size and grandeur with Asheville, North Carolina's Biltmore House (claims status as "Most visited house in America").

Most Newport mansions are now open to the public and are considered historical markers. Some, too, continue as private residences, but they're in the distinct minority, and some live by a sweet negotiation whereby some sections are open to the public, while other portions remain private.

Ticket sales offset the cost of maintenance and taxes. The very rich, today, determined it's just too expensive to flaunt their opulence.

But what does Newport have to do with Asheville?

George Washington Vanderbilt hired society architect Richard Morris Hunt, to design Biltmore House from 1888-1895. Born to the upper class, Hunt would similarly preside over construction of Vanderbilt's brothers' homes–Marble House and the Breakers, in Newport, Rhode Island, during the Gilded Age, when ostentatious living was de rigueur.

Both locations offer spectacular scenery–the mountains in one, the ocean in the other.

Asheville vs. Our Native Town, Warwick, Rhode Island

There's just something about western North Carolina's rolling hills and vistas around every corner that spoke to me. They had an air of familiarity, and that probably had a lot to do with why we bought in this region, after years of searching.

But we factored in a great deal in our decision, things we learned over many years of searching for our retirement Shangri-La.

Here are the specifics:

At last count, Asheville's 2015 population was 88,512 and growing. Females to males are almost even, though my North Carolina women friends would dispute that. Median age is 37.6, and household income is $42,558, while overall North Carolina household income is $45,906.

Only the towns of Charlotte, Greensboro-High Point, Raleigh, and Winston-Salem match Asheville's explosive growth over the past many years.

In land mass, Asheville comprises an area of forty-five square miles.

According to the website, www.city-data.com (now www.USA.com/Asheville), the town where we bought our townhome, Weaverville, 9.6

miles to the north of downtown Asheville, has a last-recorded 2014 population of 3793, of whom 51% are female and 49% are male. Household income, at $56,802, is significantly higher than North Carolina's statewide average. The value of an average home or townhome in Weaverville is $185,100, while the average state-wide value is $154,300.

A possible reason for higher household income and prices in Weaverville? New transplants to the region—like Paul and me—older folks who want the charm of a small town, with the proximity to downtown Asheville. North of Asheville is where the growth currently explodes, due to the fact the south of Asheville has been the focus of development in the past.

If the bigger town of Asheville and its little sister—Weaverville-were candidates seeking a match on a dating website site, the ad might read: "Liberal, laid-back, and looking for similar, like-minded individual. Into nature and environmental concerns, with particular emphasis on greening the planet. Close-minded individuals need not apply."

Back in Rhode Island, Paul and I live in Warwick, the second largest city in Rhode Island, one whose population is 82,670, almost identical to Asheville's, one whose median household income is $60,980, to Asheville's $56,000. According to a WalletHub Study (Dec. 3, 2017), Warwick, Rhode Island, was named 3rd safest town in the nation, based on many variables. We're in good company: Nashua, New Hampshire was 1st and South Burlington, Vermont, came in 2nd.

Warwick residents are 43,317 females to 38,646 males who enjoy a diverse culture that began as far back as the Industrial Revolution when many ethnic groups arrived to man the mills and factories. Its suburban character is reflective of its industrial past. But the city also touts thirty-nine miles of coastline, hugging the Atlantic.

By our move to Weaverville, North Carolina, Paul and I were coming from a much more densely populated region, but that was the point for our moving. We wanted a less frenzied lifestyle.

As to state statistics, at 1,214 square miles, Rhode Island runs forty-eight miles north to south and thirty-seven miles east to west. As such, it is the smallest state in the United States, half of whose borders face the ocean, hence the moniker "The Ocean State." The state's population, at last count, was 1,055,000.

But Rhode Island hasn't enjoyed the uptick in people moving into the state that North Carolina has, a reality driven by milder weather in the Southern clime and punishing taxes and metropolitan mismanagement in the Northern one.

In fact, Rhode Island is currently trying to stem the tide of exit from this state that enjoys such natural wonders. This book will attempt to answer the questions of why so many leave and why many others (like us) come back.

But my question remains: Did we ultimately choose Asheville because of the subtle way it reminded us of Rhode Island?

Who We Are

S ome people have called us "The Odd Couple" for Paul and I appear dissimilar, at first blush. He's a Southern boy raised on a cotton plantation, in Arkansas, while I grew up in a New England factory town of many mills, booming along, at full throttle, in the 40's and 50's.

For all intents and purposes, his parents were sharecroppers, despite the fact that his grandparents owned the cotton fields his family worked. His family of mother, father, and six siblings, occupied a one-room home beside the cotton field.

Since education wasn't of critical importance (except for learning life skills), he left school early to go into the trades. In other words, he never graduated from high school in the usual sense, attaining his GED and even Associate's Degree years later.

I was raised in a family where education was paramount. For that reason, I was one of the minority of women who went to college in the early 60's, following high school. Upon graduation, I went into teaching and continued in that career for the next thirty years.

Paul had been an independent, long-haul trucker who owned and operated two big rigs the earlier part of his adult life. He married and divorced twice, while I divorced one husband and buried two more, by the age of 43. In other words, we'd both been through life's wringer.

Paul came to my home state of Rhode Island, at the age of 20, when he joined the Navy Seabees, as a young man, stationed in Quonset Point, North Kingstown. He never left, to live elsewhere, except for sporadic stints to other lands, as a National Guardsman.

We met when he was 51 years old and I was 47.

In the early years, I never thought our relationship would last. I was reeling from too many personal disasters and he'd lived a maverick lifestyle on the road for long stretches. When we met, he was a correctional officer at the state prison. Since I'd had two marriages to abusive men, I recall thinking: "Oh, this time you've really hit the jackpot: He's a police officer (some are known for control issues) and he's into guns. (Paul was the captain of his National Guard pistol team; as such, he took his men to Little Rock, Arkansas, each year, for national competition.) I wasn't ready to throw my lot in, with another man, especially one with what I considered frightening credentials.

For ten years, we went together, exclusively, but lived separately, and I had no desire to modify that status quo. But that all changed on a cold December day, in 2002.

On that day, I learned I had breast cancer.

My younger daughter had come home from McGill University in Montreal, Canada, on Christmas break, and I kidded her that we'd get to accompany each other on appointments: the orthodontist for her and the annual mammogram for me.

She sailed through hers, while mine was a drawn-out, extended time when the facility got permission from my general practitioner to give me a follow-up ultrasound: several areas were suspect, contrasting greatly with my baseline and follow-up mammograms.

Following tests and biopsies, the hospital board determined the best course of action for me was mastectomy. For a second opinion, I sent my film and records to George Washington University Hospital, where my brother headed up the neurology department. Radiologists and oncologists at his hospital concurred: the breast had to go.

In the weeks ahead, my general surgeon and plastic surgeon performed mastectomy and initial reconstruction. The nine-hour surgical procedure and my adverse reaction to anesthesia landed me in the Intensive Care Unit (ICU) for three days. When I went home, Paul moved in, to care for me, guiding me in and out of the shower and providing meals—even if they were of the fast-food variety.

From that point on, we began living together, permanently.

Two years later, I wrote the Cover Story that appeared in *Providence Journal*'s "Lifestyles" Sunday magazine, documenting my diagnosis and treatment. In "I Got the News All Women Dread" (Dec. 2004), I detailed my experience so other women (and men) wouldn't be so frightened about their own breast cancer diagnosis and to encourage all to get mammograms.

Paul and I have a unique relationship built strong over time and tested with the crises we faced, but we never officially married. When others assumed our status as "married" (doctors, etc.), I never corrected, because, frankly, other things of pressing order took priority. Besides, the terms "boyfriend" or "girlfriend" seem ridiculous, at this point in our lives; "lover" hardly seems appropriate; and "friend" just doesn't cut it.

He and I have both had significant life experience; we've traveled a great deal; we've been responsible for the well-being of families. We've worked long and hard, over many years. But our commitment to each other has never wavered.

And because, as a couple, we're more "independent loners" than not, we searched for the kind of community that would allow that aspect of our personalities to flourish.

Asheville provided that....at first.

Paul and I stand before falls outside town of Highlands. Did we really wear this Ken and Barbie look-alike outfit? Mine sports logo of "Asheville Under Glass," the column I wrote as a new transplant to the region, for the popular, local newspaper, *Mountain Xpress*.

Why We're Not Naples,
Florida Folks

Years ago, we began the big journey, basically interviewing places we'd like to end up (I'm not talking "funereal," here.) Naples, Florida, was one of the destinations we checked out for retirement. With that, we went on a week-long vacation there.

I must say the beachfront villas were gorgeous; the shopping wonderful (albeit high-end, and touristy). But it wasn't for us. Here are the two prime reasons Paul and I are not Naples residents: (1.) Restaurants are jam-packed. Now, considering eating-out is practically our main priority (sorry—just being honest), that wasn't going to work for us. We don't give our name to maitre d's and we don't "tip big" to move our names up a long queue.

Furthermore, we never wait (oh, maybe ten minutes at Marco's Pizza, on Merrimon Ave., in Asheville), but that's only because we chat with the owner, while we wait.

So, waiting there is social engagement–never punishment.

There's just no food that Paul and I figure is worth our spending precious time on a bench or chair. And stand in line? Get serious!

Then, too, there's another big reason:

(2.) Paul doesn't dress in acceptable fashion…or in any fashion…and least of all, not by Naples' standards. And frankly, I'd not pass muster in that quarter either. Naples' folks wear Tommy Hilfiger (he calls him Hilfinger, like he's a James Bond character) or Tommy Bahama coordinated outfits.

Sometimes if he jumps in the car, to join me on a jaunt and we decide to stop for lunch, only then do I realize he's wearing his twenty-year-old bathing suit trunks, missing the pull for the waist.

You see, he thinks they're shorts....perfectly fine ones, at that.

Last week, while doing some pruning in his real, reasonably new Tommy Hilfiger shirt, he cut himself on a thorny rosebush (he always does this), and because he didn't think he could get the bloodied mess off his sleeves, he did what any reasonable person would do—he cut the sleeves off the shirt.

Since I'd bought the shirt for him for the rare occasions he'd need something nice to wear, I went ballistic. You see, he never destroys the awful clothes he's had for decades!! That screaming eagle t-shirt with the crushed beer can in his beak has been with us forever, as has the white shirt with an Arkansas "hawg" rutting across the front of it.

They're all hanging neatly in his closet...But the ragged remains of TH stare at me, daily, from our shared closet.

But I can't make this column all about him, for I'd have trouble in Naples, too.

Naples women dress smartly and elegantly. They wear Jimmy Choo shoes and carry Louis Vuitton bags (the real ones—not the knock-offs.) Their jewelry is real gold and their watches are Rolex. In short, they scream "Wealth." They've arrived...and they not only arrive...they pull up in Rolls-Royce...give the keys to the valet...and sail in to meet their many friends, post-tennis.

They don't really "do the beach" (too aware of age spots and skin cancer), for that sandy strip is really more like an accompaniment or an accessory...It's there, to look good, or as perfect backdrop.

Like the residents.

In contrast, most Ashevillians never really care how they look.... The older ones figure they suited up all through life and now, they're blessedly free from dress constraints. The younger ones most likely never cared...

So that's it, in a nutshell...The reasons we found Asheville so inviting.

Here's a tee shirt Paul wears often. It wouldn't pass muster in Naples.

Love at First Sight
(OK, Maybe Not "First")

We Buy a Townhome

We fell in love...or rather, I fell in love.

The stone dwellings at Hamburg Crossing, on Reems Creek, in Weaverville, reminded me of the charming cottages I'd seen dotting the English countryside. The looming mountain backdrop insured my belief: we'd found our retirement home. We'd been in the Asheville region four days.

My younger daughter told me later: "I recommended Asheville to you years earlier but you never listened." I told her: "I was recovering from breast cancer and had no reason to think I'd even be around to enjoy my retirement years. It's understandable your recommendation fell on deaf ears."

Now, four years after breast cancer, I was ready to commit to the belief I'd enjoy a future.

We narrowed our search to townhomes in three communities. The first complex, set high on a hill in the rolling countryside near Black Mountain, another sweet little town in the region, enjoyed a wonderful location, overlooking a valley, a cluster community of townhome cottages, beautifully appointed with trees, perennials, rock walls, etc. We spoke to residents and asked how they liked it there. The consensus was, "Oh, we love waking up to this every day...beautiful scenery, great group of people, etc."

The problem for me? Two factories below. I'd seen hulking behemoths visually pollute my own town's landscape when the host industry abandoned a mill. Since we couldn't know the future of the industries in question, we passed on that community.

The Orchards, outside of Hendersonville, was a considerable undertaking whose builder model was displayed in the sales office. When we visited, at the height of the booming real estate market, it was at the early stages of its development. Since we were newcomers to the region, I asked the young agent: "What's the difference between Hendersonville and Weaverville?" (the two towns that hosted the townhome communities we considered).

She responded: "Oh, there's just no comparison between the two. Hendersonville is *the place* to be for excitement. It's got a ton going on."

This young woman had spoken her preference. She never realized we'd left the busy corridors of the Northeast for the opposite–a quieter lifestyle.

We settled on Hamburg Crossing, in the little town of Weaverville whose best assets were: (1.) an under-ten-mile proximity to downtown Asheville, with the excitement we might occasionally want; (2.) entrance to the Blue Ridge Parkway, a mere five miles down the road; and (3.) Well-Bread Bakery, a New York style eatery famed for its delicious confections, light lunch and dinner fare (I told you that eating is important to us).

As proposed buyers of a townhome in this community, we had one option—the model, the one-floor Canterbury style we preferred. All others were sold. We negotiated back and forth a couple of times, through our realtor, modestly increasing our bid, but the builder refused to budge.

In recognition of the wise realtor adage of "Never love a property too much," we walked away.

Over the next several days, our realtor sent us pictures of a possible alternate choice in the same community. A two-story Villa II was coming on the market. Its original buyers had defaulted when they couldn't sell their Florida home, a contingency to their purchase. This unit was larger than most; it had a great view (in my opinion, the best in the complex) from its second floor. That view is what sold me. The buyers had already paid for upgrades of an upstairs wall and a door to close off the formerly open loft, a separate heating and cooling control (apart from the main one on the first floor) in the upstairs suite, and an extra row of maple cabinets in the kitchen.

Its strong points were: a southern exposure, insuring much sunlight; it was off the central loop, meaning we'd not have the foot traffic from those who daily walk their dogs (dog owners might prefer the center loop); it didn't face a berm or a wall. Because it was situated in the second row in from Reems Creek Road, traffic noise from the main road was lessened. We checked with residents: the units, though sharing common walls, were quiet (in Paul's condo in Rhode Island, one could hear a toilet flush in the next-door unit). Hamburg Crossing enjoyed thick fire walls.

Our offer was accepted and we went under contract. In the negotiating, I mandated the builder put in granite counters of black with amber thread, as opposed to the green granite he planned on using. We'd get a credit for the wall-to-wall carpeting, already installed, on the first floor, a credit we'd use toward hardwoods floors we'd put in. Everything negotiated was written down.

What would I do differently in future? Hire an inspection professional knowledgeable in North Carolina building for the walk-thru, for though I am a professional realtor, I couldn't know the builders' code for the region, nor could I know building issues that might affect our investment. An independent inspector would have been able to assess the level of builder competency and warn us of possible pitfalls.

As it was, we were fortunate.

As the last buyers into the complex, we lucked out, too, for full ownership meant the Home Owners' Association (HOA) monthly maintenance fee for trash pick-up, lawn maintenance, and the capital fund would enjoy stability. Since these units were brand new, we didn't need to ask about capital fund stability to handle future needs in the community (wall/foundation/roof repair... painting, etc.) As a realtor, I know the health of the capital fund is of major importance in older communities where repairs will need to be done.

With that, we went into sales agreement for our Hamburg Crossing home.

Townhome/Condo Living

In our first year, in Asheville, everything was new and fresh. Including friends.

People who had migrated from all over the country, nested with fervor, and our townhome community seemed to have a disproportionate number of new owners from Maine, Michigan, and the states where winters are harsh.

We were all excited with the prospect of getting to know one another, and thanks to a socially skilled woman who initiated all social gatherings, we enjoyed regular theme dinners (St. Patrick's Day, Easter), while Yoga classes, book clubs, and recitals came to us.

Another woman set up monthly get-togethers called Lunch Bunch, whereby we community residents met at the clubhouse, car-pooled, and visited restaurants in the region.

Group outings were planned and communal hikes to nearby destinations were led by those who were native North Carolinians familiar with the territory.

But, as is often the case, with these social events, some residents did all the work, while others sat back and enjoyed the fruits of others' labor.

Rancor developed over time; the woman who managed social gatherings quit, and we all discovered: she wasn't easily replaced. Then, too, cliques developed.

As the years ticked on, Paul and I noted patterns that seemed to develop—the same that seemingly occur in group or townhome/condominium communities everywhere.

And because Paul and I were part-time residents, living back in Rhode Island for seven months at a time, only to return for five, we noted dramatic changes in friends when we returned.

Some were diagnosed with terrible diseases; others appeared to age profoundly; a few suffered devastating losses due to financial mistakes or death of partners. Those whose newly single situation posed financial hardship had to take on part-time jobs to make ends meet, etc.

Their lifestyle changed, remarkably.

It was as if we first residents of this new community who'd begun life there with such bright hopes had them dashed with life's harsher realities.

Then, too, as we all aged, we became a community of mostly single women, many of whom ultimately traded husbands and partners for pets as companions.

Deaths occurred regularly.

At times, I'd say to Paul, as I gazed out to a community whose shuttered blinds kept out the sun and the spectacular view of the mountains: "I wonder what they do all day?" Most had no jobs or were of an age where intense activity was limited.

Those who had dogs walked them along the central circle of homes, several times a day. On those occasions, they connected with other women and traded the latest news on the community.

Sometimes, we residents combined social occasions with solemnity.

On one such day, we had not merely traveled the winding route to Mount Mitchell for lunch. Our line of five or six cars snaked along the many small, off-shoot roads, searching for familiar signs that told our lead vehicle she'd found her destination.

We were there to pay our respects to the husband of one of the women of our complex, on the first anniversary of her scattering of his ashes.

Only problem? She couldn't find him.

So, we got out and she looked, hoping a tree, a rock promontory would kick on a memory. His widow felt this was the place but she was unsure. After an uncomfortable silence, she shared that it was probably all right to not know the exact spot, because, after all, she did cast Edward's ashes to the four winds atop Mt. Mitchell, in the first place.

That said, he could be anywhere in the vicinity....

You see, she'd lost her point of reference. Why? Road crews had moved the roadway canister that she mentally noted as marker for the general area where she'd scattered him.

She reasoned that there'd be no one more amused than her Edward, the subject of our hunt. He'd enjoy the sheer hilarity of watching a parade of older folks endlessly circling a mountain top, to honor one of their own...searching, yet unable to find him.

Hard-living, motorcycle-riding Edward loved flying under the radar.

And I'd note: We seniors are a motley group, at all points in the aging process. Our oldest, a 92-year-old man always amazed us: He joined Paul and me at our gym (in the clubhouse) daily, even if he performed his athletic routine on a stationary bike "Mr. Magoo fashion," at the slowest revolutions.

He was the barometer that told us what we'd all face—if we were lucky.

Meanwhile, each year brought fresh assaults that reminded us to live fully each day. There was our nimble bicyclist neighbor who suffered a stroke on a three-state marathon bike trip. He was an athlete who prepped endlessly, for he was no mere weekend warrior on the roadways.

At 66, he succumbed to a genetic fault he knew nothing about.

There are the crop of new widows who've seen husbands of many years cut down or others newly diagnosed with life-altering illnesses.

Whatever. Their lives are inextricably altered.

There is no place quite so dramatic for life changes as a townhome community whose residents are mostly seniors.

Word to the wise: When you cast off a partner or friend, choose immovable markers, unless you really want one's final resting place to be literally "up in the air."

The following is an account of one of our first hikes in the region, demonstrating our zest for life in our new land and appreciation of new friends in our complex.

HCHC: Hamburg Crossing Hiking Club First Hike

Today was a fine hike, indeed, as the group trekked a wooded trail skirting a stream that had seen headier days. We were all properly suited up in long pants (lest we attract chiggers and ticks), hats, bug spray, and ever-important walking sticks (a requisite fashion item now that a pesky bear has been spotted in our compound!).

Our little group followed our leader who had knowledge of these local trails, noting nature, wildflowers, and berries wherever appropriate. When one of the group noticed an abandoned hummingbird nest, we all sprang into action, fastening those selfsame walking sticks into tools to attain the treasure. After several moments of artful juxtaposition of bodies and devices, we managed to recover the artifact, intact, much to the delight of its new owner. It's hopefully labeled and housed in a proper showcase, attesting to the earliest forays of our feisty group whose collective spirit brought down our quarry.

The wooded habitat provided clues of earlier homesteading in the ram-shackle cabins that stood, while the stream bed gave evidence of decades of the river's usual power that polished the rocks to a smooth alabaster. Along the banks, blackberries grew in abundance and our group reveled in pick-ing them, avoiding the poison ivy, while a hawk signaled his displeasure by shooting up through the branches of a tree, alarmed by our presence.

On the return, however, our group fell into disarray as Paul led the men down towards the rocky stream, leaving us women on the trail. For the next several moments, the men became boys again, investigating the hiding places of the river, skipping rocks, looking for elusive fish in swirling eddies and pools. Finally, the boys/men tired of the play and rejoined us, as we all headed in one lane toward the parking lot for our new focus—lunch.

We followed a winding dirt trail to our next location, along the banks of the French Broad River, where we planned to picnic, beside the rushing river.

I strode ahead of the group to one of the vacant tables (it's Monday on a clear, cool day), but as I approached, I saw a pouch-like something on the cement platform on which the table stood. It was a man's billfold, bulging with money! I looked around but saw no one.

As the rest of the group arrived, I shared the news of what I'd found, and as I looked through the billfold, I noted one ID card that simply read "Senior Citizen" where a person's name should have been. We all laughed. Finally, I found the driver's license. The owner was a Tennessee-an to whom I'd ship the billfold.

After a half hour of shared fun and good eating (one woman shared her bag of mini Snickers candies), we determined it was time to head back. As we walked to our cars, an older vehicle pulled up, with a nervous man, driving, and a woman who was so wound up that she leapt out of the car. Two children (grandkids?) were in the back seat. He nervously asked: "Did any of you happen to see a man's wallet?"

And just to be assured this wallet belonged to this man, I asked: "And what does this wallet look like?"(it was engraved with a couple dancing). The man replied: "Oh, it's something bluegrass....that's all my family ever gets me." It was close enough—I'd found my man, the owner of the plump billfold. They left—one happy family. He tried to give me a reward, something my hiking mates kept refusing—on my behalf.

It was a lovely way to spend a day, cavorting through the North Carolina countryside, enjoying great conversation, eating, and insuring one lucky man survived another day.

There is infinite goodness in our corner of the world.

Friend-Making in a New Land

Many years ago a movie based on author Mary McCarthy's book, *The Group,* tracked the lives of a tight-knit group of eight women who'd gone to a Vassar-like college. After graduation, they went their separate ways, only to be brought back together for the funeral of one of them. The movie touched on the many hot-button social issues affecting women in this period of the 30's.

My eclectic Asheville women friends remind me of this group, for they're "so Asheville."

We had all come to Asheville, at approximately the same time, some nine years ago, so it begs the question: "Was there a cosmic pull that simply affected all of us, at the same moment in history?"

Who's in our band of merry-makers? One woman cheered on her quadriplegic son in Sochi, Russia, in his quest for gold at the Paralympics some years back. The rest of the time she runs three thriving businesses. Next, there's a massage therapist who lives in Asheville and has another home in Florida, one she bought at the top of the market and now rents out; a government worker with an impressive security clearance; a performer who lends her acting and singing skills to theatrical ventures about town; an accountant; a floral arranger.

Some, like me, live in two states, though they go the more traditional route that puts them in warmer climes than North Carolina, in winter.

Two of our group are coming off thirty-plus year marriages. They distance themselves from former lives and try to create new ones. One told me: "For all these years, I've raised children and facilitated my husband. Now, I want to find out who I am and what I can do." At 50-plus, they join a job market, swollen with out-of-work young people, yet we cheer them on, for most of us have seen our own marriages wrecked on the rocks of divorce or have been victims of widowhood.

Younger ones in our group wisely listen, realizing they'll be on the next platform of life. Besides, we lace our gatherings with humor and raucous laughter.

We encourage each other to be individualistic, go after what each wants to take their talents and considerable gifts of a lifetime and try to figure a way to make money from these.

Asheville's encouraging that way. It's a land of many people on later life paths, sort of in keeping with a card (also the product of an Asheville woman) that read something to the effect of "Keep your really good girlfriends...." On the inside, it reads "They'll be in your life a lot longer than husbands."

So true. How do I know? I've burned through three partners and I'm currently on the fourth, even if he has been with me, now, for twenty-five years.

How'd I get this gang of women? When Paul and I first moved to Asheville, I missed girlfriends back home, so when a woman I'd met at a newcomer meeting, invited me to a group gathering (Asheville's all about networking), I jumped at the chance of bonding with other women.

I wasn't disappointed. Our group is an eclectic mix, similar to the demographic that comes to Asheville. We're comprised of: mostly white, one African-American, a Southerner by birth, two gays, one vegan, two divorced, one wishing she were, two others sharing domicile with men (though they're not the much-touted "friends with benefits") and then, there's me.

I'm the oldest, a fact of which one (next oldest) reminds us all, whenever age is mentioned. Our youngest is in her late 40's. I think she's fortunate, indeed, for having older women as friends, for she taps into the experience and collective wisdom, as she heads down paths many of us have already trod.

Four have full-time careers, with two launched on a new career path. One left a long-term marriage and now shares her husband's 401k, pension, and benefits accrued over a lifetime, despite the fact that was never that husband's plan.

Two of our group never married.

Because I'm a thirty-year, retired teacher, I get a pension and live with a mate who also gets a steady retirement income from the three careers he had.

As a group, we used to meet at restaurants but when our howling laughter kept others from enjoying their meal, we moved our get-togethers to our homes.

We celebrate the big events in our lives: birthdays, arrival of grandchildren, new jobs, divorces, new living arrangements. And we give support when appropriate, as when one of us went through a spate of losses in quick succession.

We are a veritable font of talent, perfectly willing to share with each other what we've learned on this journey.

We're dangerously inventive. When one of us wanted to go on a shared-expense (and nothing else) trip to Europe and others of our group couldn't go, she put an ad, requesting a travel mate, on Craigslist, and a man responded. They took that trip together.

To this day, we marvel at the insanity of such an impromptu match.

The above is a picture of our women's group at my "Leaving Asheville Party," held at Stoney Knob restaurant, in Weaverville. I'm seated, in the center.

Friend-Losing in a New Land:
"Rest in Peace, Ralph..."

Many townhome communities are probably mostly made up of seniors or those decidedly not-young, those who are newly settling in a region touted for its popularity among an older demographic. When one lives in such a community, she notes much ebb and flow of residents: those who found the lifestyle didn't match their expectations; others who missed grandchildren in their state of origin, or those whose compromised health saw them go to assisted living or nursing facilities. Then, too, there were those who died.

Occasionally, a young family with children moved into our townhome community, but they were the exception, and they became almost mascots for our group. A child's tricycle or skateboard was a rarity in our neighborhood. Mostly, we were a band of older folks.

Our social gatherings ran the gamut of group breakfasts, luncheons at local restaurants, hospital visits, and attendance at funerals for a community member.

With regard to the last, I have noted over my lifetime that in funeral attendance, I discover aspects of folks' lives I never knew before. Such was the case with one legendary member of our Hamburg Crossing community.

116

Our deceased friend had been Assistant Postmaster General for the United States who had risen in the ranks. He was 86 years old when he died, following an almost-idyllic life he'd shared with his wife of sixty-four years.

Ralph and Vi met in elementary school; they had two sons and three grandchildren.

He was a funny man who told acceptable (never cringe-worthy) jokes at our socials.

Because of that, I knew he'd appreciate what happened when Paul and I went to his funeral. I knew others would appreciate the story, too.

Here's how it played out:

We got up early that Saturday morning (7:00 A.M.). Our plan was to go to the funeral home first, pay our respects to the family (this is the practice in New England), and then go to the 11:00 A.M. service at United Central Methodist church, in downtown Asheville. I had looked up the information regarding Ralph's service on the internet.

As we drove along Patton Ave, in Asheville, before 10:00 A.M., I saw a church sign and sang out, "There's Central United Methodist." I mistakenly believed the cars entering the parking lot were advance staff from the funeral home.

When we got to Groce Funeral Home, we found an empty lot. A young man dressed in a business suit came over to our car, asking if he could help, to which I replied, "Is Ralph (last name) here? We're paying our respects to the family."

"No, I'm sorry," he said: "I believe he's at our Lake Julian facility, but I'll check."

He returned, with a man who said: "The family buried Mr..... this morning...It was private. The church service is at 11:00 A.M., at United Central Methodist."

We left, thinking, "We'll grab a coffee and then head over to the church." It was 10:00 A.M.

At 10:45 A.M., we went to the church, parked in the lot, and proceeded inside.

But when we came through the doors, the Spanish-speaking congregants all stared at us. Finally, a man at the podium quit his station and came up to us, asking: "Can I be of help?"

"Yes," we offered, "We thought our friend's funeral was here, but we realize it isn't."

He offered it might be at the *other* United Methodist Church— in downtown Asheville, on Church Street.

Hurriedly, I coursed the back streets of downtown Asheville, looking for a parking spot (never easy on a Saturday). When I found one, characterized by a disabled meter with a yellow sticker on it, I took it. I didn't even care if a meter person ticketed me (they're quick to do that, in Asheville). At 11:05 A.M., we were now, officially "late."

We went toward a door that looked like a church entrance, but the woman told us "No, the main building is up there, where the columns are."

"Of course, it is," I thought inwardly.

We trudged up the hill, went through serpentine corridors, heard voices below, followed the stairway down, only to find ourselves right back where we encountered that same woman. This time, she offered: "I'm sorry for all your trouble. Here, I'll take you."

She led us back up the stairs and down a hallway where she opened a door. Finally, we saw people we knew. We were at Ralph's funeral.

That's where we heard what a multi-dimensional person Ralph was.

But we knew, too: He would've loved knowing our crazy efforts to find his funeral.

He would've enjoyed even more, knowing something else....

In the darkness of early day, Paul had taken a pair of black slacks from our shared closet.

Only hours later, he wondered, "Why's the hook on these pants on the other side?"

When I pulled back the inside waistband, I saw the familiar DKNY (Donna Karan, New York, an upscale women's line) label.

Paul had attended Ralph's funeral, wearing my slacks. Even worse—They looked better on him than they do on me!

Yes, Ralph would have truly loved this....

Upshot to this article: When in the South, know in advance that there are many varieties of Methodist and Baptist churches.

It would behoove one to know exact destination of a funeral service ahead of time.

Franklin's Caffe Rel, Friends' Mountain Retreat, and Treasure-Hunting

I'll warrant that in any first year of any new residential community, the residents are excited to investigate their new surroundings. In fact, Paul and I were on continual ventures of discovery, visiting towns and villages all over, either with a group or as a couple. Distance was never a deterrent.

The following was a typical planned event for our tribe. We traveled one glorious fall day, in high hopes of capturing a superior (and reasonable) meal at Caffe Rel (spelled 2 f's by choice), in Franklin, North Carolina. We later planned to enjoy coffee and dessert comprised of apples from a local orchard, at the mountain retreat of our townhome neighbors, Pat and Larry.

At Caffe Rel, we were early enough to get the much-sought-after tables. What did we order? She-crab bisque ("magnifique,") grouper for some, heavenly pot roast with julienned vegetables, in creamy gravy, a delectable salmon, salads, etc.

Chef Rel has Cordon Bleu training; as a result, a long line of ardent fans snakes out the door, from 11:30 A.M. on.

He appears all contradictions, as he runs about in French beret, in his truck stop-type diner, while his late-model Porsche sits just outside the front door. When I asked if he'd been written up by Gourmet magazine, he chuckled that his eaterie had garnered a review in the North Carolina magazine *Our State,* as "a wonderful surprise in the back country."

He's refreshing, too, in that he never attempts political correctness: "You must be this big to eat here" is the placard cut-out that appears on his website, discouraging parents from bringing their too-young children to his establishment.

We skipped the fabulous desserts (one was a mountainous three-layer-that-looked-like-eight chocolate cake, beckoning from its glass encasement on the counter), since we were next en route to our friends' cabin, for dessert.

Our hosts led the way, while we followers were advised to stay close. I had earlier asked, "But what's the street address, in case we get lost?" Pat replied, "There is none!" I then said, "All right, then what's your cell number, so we can call you if we get separated?" Pat looked shocked: "We don't have a cell. It wouldn't matter if we did. There are no cell towers."

I picked up my incredulity and got back into the car, intent on following our hosts right to the edges of Hell, if need.

Their lead vehicle proceeded up the mountain, on a road that acted very much like the infamous, serpentine "Tail of the Dragon" road in Tennessee. When the road narrowed and the pavement ceased, we negotiated a rough, rutted terrain and on one occasion, wrestled a good five minutes with another car coming from the opposite direction, until he ceded us the right of way. He was outnumbered: three cars to his one. But we continued on, because this is what North Carolinians apparently do, to enjoy their mountainside retreats.

Finally, at the top, we praised our friends' delightful hideaway, jam-packed with their famed love of all things "comfort." Hidden away in nooks and crannies were a treasure trove of delights: family artifacts and pictures of Larry and Pat in former years, along with a lifetime of wonderful memories.

The garage satisfied all the more, and other Hamburg Crossing resident, 92-year-old Ken, managed to find himself a seat on a golf cart (doesn't everyone have one of these in their garage?), while we all rummaged through, singing out each time we found something remarkable (the biggest ceramic piggy bank!), old shutters lined against a wall, candelabra, pots, and pans.

Following our cabin sojourn, we drove to the nearby town of Cashiers (pronounced Cash/iers, as opposed to how one pronounces cash register clerks at supermarkets), where we gushed again, this time over the gorgeous lakeside home-furnishing emporium where many of us bought souvenirs of our day.

Finally, we ambled home, with a plan for our next outing.

Some of us have expressed real interest in one neighbor's llama farm as next trip. THAT would be interesting, too.

Thrash About?...Keep Still?...

Anyone new to a region needs to apprise himself of conditions that will affect his safety and well-being. When living in territory like western North Carolina (or anywhere, for that matter), it behooves one to know what wildlife shares terrain with humans.

For instance, it was never a good idea to hang hummingbird feeders out the window of one's Western North Carolina townhome because bears are attracted to the saccharine liquid (remember, they're the same ones who like honey), hence the bird feeder prohibition in many communities.

I always forget the appropriate admonition. I'm talking about what one is supposed to do if she finds herself suddenly in the path of a bear. It's important because such a chance encounter can easily happen in the woodlands of North Carolina or in many other regions of the United States.

I suspect that I'll be the one who forgets what to do and piss some bear off—royally. Just like I fear when we're back in our home state, frolicking in the ocean waters of Rhode Island, suddenly finding myself, jaw to jaw with....well... "Jaws."

Do I thrash about or remain calm (as if that's possible in this type of situation!)?

Yes, I know the part about gouging the shark's eyes out but let's face it, that kind of focus will take serious concentration, as well as a deft blow to the pupil region. I doubt I'll be able to pull off such, when I'm in a panic situation, screaming and churning water.

OK, the same rule of "what to do?" confounds me here, in North Carolina, regarding bears. Which rule to follow? Do I thrash about and make noise? Do I try to remain mute?

It's important because Paul and I like to go hiking along trails— trails I know bears are probably hiking as well.

That's the reason a few years back in Asheville I bought a contraption-a bell on a wrist strap (they sold it at a tourist store, so I know my fear is one shared by many).

Or maybe bear contraption marketers figure we new residents are gullible.

According to instructions attached to this device, the hiker is supposed to strap on the bell wristlet during woodland jaunts, in case she encounters a post-hibernating bear who's ravenous and isn't fussy about what he eats...as long as it fills him up.

The bell alerts him to the fact the person is approaching and so the bear avoids said hiker altogether (or so the ad implies). He'll supposedly run off and hide.

Well, that's if he's a normal bear. My concern? What if he isn't? Specifically, what if he's dysfunctional, dyslexic (and confuses directions), or psychopathic?

On another score, I can't recall what color fur signifies herbivorous and carnivorous bears. Oh, I know the white ones are polar. They're easy...I know they like to eat humans. Grizzlies, too. They've got the kind of hair color I used to have when I was young—chestnut or auburn. Since they've got that reddish tinge, it's easier for me to remember. They're hot-tempered (like all redheads); they're definitely meat-eaters. Hell, the name "Grizzly" even implies they're not affectionate.

But brown bears? Hmmm...I had a teddy bear once, a sweet, cuddly thing, when I was a little girl, and he was a chocolate brown.

Come to think of it, however, I recall this brown bear behind a high cage at Grandfather Mountain—definitely a carnivore, otherwise he'd be in the petting zoo.

We know size has got nothing to do with it, as we see with those lovable, large Panda bears who are docile creatures. They're pure leaf-eaters...

But black bears (the kind in the Asheville woods)...well, I think they're probably laid-back vegans, like a huge part of the population in this town, meaning they prefer a non-meat diet. They probably don't have a mean or nasty bone in their bodies. They're purists at heart but then again, I'm not sure they're "absolute purist." I mean, you take a ravenous, vegan, berry-eater, leaf-finisher out of his cave after a several month hiatus and dangle a hunk of human flesh in front of him/her (me on a path in the woods), I'm just not sure he'll remain true to his principles.... Just like real vegans in Asheville, if confronted with real starvation.

So, make noise or go quietly into the woods? Carry the damned bell strap or toss it aside?

Hell, if I heard all this noise (the bells) in my habitat, I might attack the interloper out of sheer annoyance.

Just trying to see it from the bear's perspective...

Quick Take on Towns Outside Asheville

Towns outside Asheville bespeak America's former glory. Mars Hill, Marshall, Burnsville, and Spruce Pine come to mind for having all seen busier days, at least in winter. The lumber yard's pallets, in Spruce Pine, remain empty—and rusty railroad tracks sit silent, no doubt wondering where all the fun and travelers went.

Warehouses are empty reminders of their heyday, when they housed products they were initially built for.

Streets are relatively unpopulated, except for occasional visitors who try to get a handle on the region. In these towns are often one or two art galleries, where local artisans display their wares, and there's almost always an occasional coffee shop or luncheon bistro.

But the bustle (at least in the five months of the year we were there) is missing.

Because we were "Reverse Halfbacks," a term I coined for our living in the region when other Asheville-ites go to Florida (to get away from the cold and to enable their six months and a day residence requirement to become Sunshine state legits), we have a half-baked perception of the region, so I claim no expertise on the other months.

It is specifically for the reason that we live in Asheville during the tough season (and not the tourist one) that I tried, every year, unsuccessfully, to get Biltmore Estate to allow us two-state winter residents a discount. I mean: How many times does one need or want to visit Biltmore House itself? Furthermore, we never got the real bang for our significant outlay for a season pass, since we were gone during the time when Biltmore offered outdoor, summer-time, musical occasions.

But I digress....

Here's my take on peripheral towns, none of which is supposed to be read as gospel, though we did spend significant time in these realms (the following are in no particular order of importance).

Two such towns–Cashiers and Highlands enjoy the natural beauty of their surrounding countryside and have become meccas for the well-heeled from elsewhere who shop upscale or golf well-groomed greens; Waynesville's got a fabulous Greek restaurant whose grilled chicken on green salad we go miles for (it's got cute shops, too); Brevard has interesting antique shops and the elusive white squirrels which we've actually seen and which make their domicile on the grounds of the music school, so they're obviously music lovers and animals with good taste; Hot Springs the heated waters, tubs, and bathing suits to borrow, if you didn't bring one or are too shy to go in the buff; Cherokee's got gambling; Maggie Valley's got ski resorts though we never saw much snow, compared to New England standards; Franklin's got the best 5-star restaurant in a gasoline/convenience store setting; Bryson City a railroad and more shops; Blowing Rock's filled with tourists and après-ski; Weaverville had us and the charms mentioned aforehand; Barnardsville's got treetops, chasms, and zip-lining; Black Mountain touts the best mushroom soup I ever ate (the Veranda Restaurant); Mars Hill has a university and top-tier visiting speakers (Maya Angelou spoke there,) Burnsville has a great crafts and art festival of 150 artisans that I've never seen, Saluda's got one of the oldest mercantiles still in operation and a shop that sells confetti glass created by a real glassblower whose studio is in Jamestown, Rhode Island; Flat Rock's got Carl Sandburg, Canton's got a real, honest-to-God, still-working paper mill, Dillsboro's got the fun Great Smoky Railroad that goes back and forth to Bryson City (we rode it); Hendersonville showcases artisan diversity in painting, woven goods, wood carving; Chimney Rock boasts Lake Lure and a rock promontory that allows great viewing; Tryon has an impressive art community; Sylva hosts the Greening Up the Mountain street festival in spring. (My apologies if your town didn't make the cut. It wasn't intentional; these are just the ones we visited most.)

And there's much beyond, too, if you day-trip out of Asheville. Lake Fontana's thirty-five miles out of Bryson City and suggests "discovery" in another realm, as in its lake, created by the Works Progress Administration (WPA) supposedly covers an abandoned town (or did the young man who told me this make up this story?). Then, there's the hairpin turns of "Tale of the Dragon" in Tennessee, where one hundred and thirty-five turns in a fifteen mile stretch of road make for pretty amazing nausea. We traveled it on one occasion, with Paul wishing he had his BSA motorcycle, joining the hordes of others on those metal beasts. He needn't have worried. In the opening mile, our muffler fell off our Volkswagen Cabrio, thus giving her an uncharacteristic growl, enabling us to compete with the two-wheeled wonders.

Another crazy aspect? In another instance of American entrepreneurial talent, on Tail of the Dragon curves, local entrepreneurs set up cameras and takes photos, selling those same at the base of the run (just like cruise personnel take pictures of guests in supposed fun activities and then sell those photos to guests).

There's Dolly Parton-ville (Pigeon Forge) and Gatlinburg's strip of amusements, in nearby Tennessee, that hopefully will recover, after the fires of the fall, if you can make it through the miles-long, roadway through-the-mountains-approach, with your queasiness in check.

Beyond all that are the lovely coastal towns of Beaufort and Charleston and further still, Savannah, Georgia.

In other words, the region is a smorgasbord of quirkiness, a true jumping-off place to investigate other destinations. Humor abounds in these mountain towns.

Below, is a truck with a sense of humor in Spruce Pine (when saying the town's name, run the two words together fast, as in Spruce-Pine).

And the elusive white squirrel, on the grounds of the Music School, in Brevard, so much a feature of Brevard that the town actually names a festival in its honor.

The Precipitous Learning
Curve of "Reverse Halfbacks"

All around our townhouse community, in winter, are houses awaiting their milder-season owners, with blinds drawn, heat set at barely above freezing to insure pipes don't burst, homes that look lonely.

Occasionally, we saw a stoic full-time resident who stepped out to take the air, joining forces with the Pet Club who dutifully walked their furry companions, each day, regardless of frigid temperatures. But we're not fooled: this group never elects this activity; it is done out of necessity. They smile and beckon to one another, willing each other to join in a walk about the compound, pretending to enjoy the exercise, while we know they seek solace in the companionship of others; it takes the sting out of the cold.

When we walk to the clubhouse for our daily exercise on the treadmills, we are met with occasional "Hi's" from baffled others who call out, "You must be Northerners to be out in this weather!" (We don't have a pet.) We find it amusing because cold as it is in North Carolina, it pales in comparison to winter temperatures back home. We are hardy souls, used to extreme weather, the kind that insulates one for six months or more, the kind of winter weather that kicks on furnaces for twenty-four hours, at a clip.

What we who prefer North Carolina weather in winter can't endure are long days and nights of extreme heat in more Southern realms, only made bearable by continuous air-conditioning.

As folks who come to town when other seasonal residents leave, we are very important for Asheville and the state of North Carolina, because we help support the local economy at the critical time when fair-weather residents quit the region, in quest of warmer climes.

We're the ones who patronize the restaurants; we shop in the big box stores or little specialty boutiques; we gas up at the local stations, and we buy our groceries (when we're not eating out) at the local Ingles, Greenlife, and Earth Fare. And we have finally gotten the message that road trips around here offer unique challenges, and one shouldn't necessarily take a route, just because it's there—not even if one has a GPS.

Case in point: Hot Springs. Some years ago, on a Sunday, we left Weaverville for Hot Springs. We thought we had enough gas for the journey and didn't bother to fuel up, because after all, we figured we'd access a gas station along the way. That's a decidedly New-England mindset that expects an open gas station on every corner (even on Sunday).

Oh, we made the trip, but barely, due to the fact there simply were no gas stations in transit, nor in the town center, itself. We were advised that a proprietor on the outskirts of town "might be open" on that Sunday. Running on vapors, we pulled in and gassed up, realizing how close we'd come to being stuck for the night. This taught us a lesson: fuel up before any drive-especially on Sundays and especially in the mountains.

In another nod to the "Things are different here" category, Paul and I recently went on a day's excursion to Spruce Pine. After visiting the town, he determined we'd go back a different route for its alternate scenery. Paul never fears getting lost, because after all, we have a GPS, and that device told us our home was a mere fourteen miles away.

So, he veered off and followed Rt. 197. For a while, all went well. Then, we both noted a significant thinning of habitation, with only an occasional home dotting the hillside. The day grew late and the sun sat low on the horizon. After about forty-five minutes of slow steady ascent, the blacktop suddenly disappeared and the asphalt road disintegrated into gravel, further complicated by patches of ice and snow. We were high up, at this point, hence the climate change. Paul sought to placate my concerns by telling me, "We're not really in trouble because power lines are still visible, suggesting civilization," while I quipped, "What do you mean, still in civilization?" I'd seen the "No trespassing" signs that didn't invite wayward travelers. The sky was ominous; ice patches grew ever more menacing; and hairpin turns were everywhere.

What our GPS didn't tell (or we simply didn't know how to use it, optimally) was the grade or condition of the projected itinerary between where we were and home. Yes, the distance was fourteen miles, but it was demanding terrain. So, a trip that should have taken a half hour, ended up taking way longer.

Following the descent, we now knew another truth about winter in our new region: up in those hills, the character of the terrain and the weather can change in an instant and pockets of precipitation are the rule, rather than the exception. And fourteen miles can be significantly different, depending on the character of those miles.

Another lesson in hill country.

Bliss for a While...
Then Another Kind of Crash

It's the same thing, really, as is the unnatural, rosy period of a new marriage... new community...or new job. The initial timeframe is so fraught with high hopes that it's even referenced when new presidents take office, a time when they face no real challenges. They haven't yet needed to negotiate differences with Congressional members.

This unnatural timeframe when all seemingly get along is called the "Honeymoon Period."

The same level of cooperation operates within a new town-home community. At first, everyone gets along. Then, dominant personalities emerge and infighting begins.

As a part-time resident, I recognized the enormous contribution of those who stepped forward to lead, in the early days of Hamburg Crossing. They took on a considerable work load with little guarantee their efforts would be appreciated. But I recognized, too: These leader types all shared a need to serve. In their youth, they served as officers or members of school student councils; as adults, they became managers or supervisors at work; as seniors, they lead their townhome communities.

Leadership appears to be in their DNA.

In my opinion, the first board of any townhome complex has the most work, since the governing rules are devised, by them, via perceived need. A ruling that says "outdoor/patio furniture must be earth tones" exists to prevent an array of discordant colors. Patio awnings aren't allowed because they fade, and then they become an eyesore. The governing body knows that aging awnings will be a problem—especially when the owner doesn't agree it needs replacement. Or it could become a liability if and when it becomes airborne.

Lawn decoration such as bloomer-exposed, bent-over ceramic ladies, pink plastic flamingoes, and blow-up Santas all make the Forbidden List of most townhome communities.

When we first moved into Hamburg Crossing, in 2006, I invited another resident who was walking by, to join me, on my patio. She happened to be on the governing board. During our brief conversation, she pointed to my ceramic bird bath (an earth tone) poised atop the flat surface of my fence, temporarily, while I determined its permanent home.

She eyed it, saying: "You know that's illegal?" (can't put garden decor on the top of the fence). She furthered the insult by adding: "And it's leaking."

She and I never became friends.

That same woman was suspected of ratting out our 80-year-old neighbor who grew a lone tomato plant on her patio. The older resident got "the letter," the one the grounds committee sends to those who break rules, advising them of their risk of fines if they don't remedy the situation. The reason for no tomato plants? Apparently, bears like tomatoes and will leave the wild in hopes of sinking their teeth into the flushy pulp of a ruby heirloom in a patio garden.

Wind chimes are forbidden (some folks apparently hate the sound) and one must seek approval, before planting of garden pots...statues...wind devices.. in the sacred mid-zone.

These are just some of the freedoms one loses in a townhome community, a fact which has driven others out. One woman missed her garden so much that she pulled up stakes (and her beloved plantings) and bought a smaller, stand-alone home nearby.

Another former board member became so disenchanted with how a thorny issue was handled that she and her husband put their unit on the market and quit our community, altogether. It all had to do with trees.

In the beginning, we residents were told we could order and pay for up to three trees we wished to plant on the little splotch of land that extended beyond our immediate patio, and we were given a list of likely tree candidates that had been approved.

With that, Paul and I purchased a birch...a red maple...and a dogwood.

Another couple bought a few of the weeping variety to be sunk into land abutting their unit and a water retention pond.

We all needed to get approval from the grounds committee before planting.

That same committee later determined the couple's weeping trees interfered with the functioning of the retention pond and the owners were told their trees had to go. A firestorm erupted. Perhaps compensation was never offered (it should have been, if the grounds committee approved their initial planting request). Warning letters were sent out.

Some time into the melee, when the owners were away, a tree removal crew came in and razed the trees, thus infuriating the owners. Shortly after, the "For Sale" sign went up, in their town-home window, and they left the community.

Back in Rhode Island, Paul and I heard about the troubles from multiple sources (which is why I'm skeptical as to who did what).

Some applied the term "Nazi squad" to the grounds committee and tensions mounted. Others left the community in sympathy mode, with some moving to a newly built community down the road which one resident sarcastically renamed "The Lost Colony."

Scuttlebutt has it that residents of that newer community suffer the same growing pains, arguing among themselves, about policies...restrictions...rules.

The question remains: Were the self-exiles mere malcontents (who complain about everything), or were they folks who needed a less restrictive community?

All I know is this: Squabbling is part of the human condition. Some folks argue about everything; others want rules just for others. In instances such as that, community living is probably not a good fit.

The bottom line? When the dissatisfied move, they take their personalities with them, like baggage. Problems arise, again, when they unpack that baggage.

But if you've been a stand-alone home resident for much of your life, you might want to consider well the pitfalls of townhome and condo living, before buying. Yes, proposed buyers must read and sign off on the by-laws and regulations governing a townhome community, but folks never quite know how those rules will impact them, until they're living under them.

Even in Asheville,
the Spiritual Goes Awry

I'm a defrocked Catholic, one of many who've drifted from the fold. For most of my life, I tried desperately to be one with my birth religion, despite serious obstacles. From my late 20's (as divorced person), I was of a group denied full participation by my church, even though my children and I attended Mass regularly.

My first husband was Baptist, raised in a rural section of the state where his father was a lay minister. That man preached on occasion when the usual circuit preacher didn't come to the little white church at the country crossroads.

But my husband and I married in the Catholic church, an action that proved my undoing.

In order for us to marry, my fiancée and I had to agree to raise our children Catholic, and we had to attend pre-Cana lessons, where we presumably learned if we were suited for life-long commitment to each other, as if a mere several week session can tell such.

But our marriage was contentious and violent, from the beginning, and I left him, in the second year, five months after the birth of our daughter. When I finally got the divorce two years later, I felt an outcast in my religion.

I was only 27 years of age.

I railed at the unfairness of a system that saw some easily attain annulments. As a single parent with no financial support from my former spouse (despite it being court-mandated), I could little afford to go through that lengthy and costly church annulment process, pressed as I was with raising my child and paying for childcare, to allow me to work.

Friends recommended I see an older priest to help me overcome my feelings of spiritual disconnection, a priest who allegedly worked wonders with another young woman in similar straits. Sympathetic to the fact I was a single parent, with a small child, he suggested we meet at my apartment, so I could avoid additional babysitter costs.

I thought him wonderfully supportive.

At my apartment, this kindly, white-bearded gentleman who could have easily been a double for Santa Claus began telling me there were many in my situation—others who felt adrift in a sea of uncertainty.

Slowly, he got into other things.

He said many young, divorced parishioners suffer sexual frustration. He asked me if I knew the church sanctioned ways to deal with such (it doesn't). He then asked me to describe, in detail, how I, a young woman, relieved my own physical urges.

At that, red flags went up and I knew him to be a voyeur, preying on my vulnerability.

I ended our meeting on the pretext I needed to pick up my child (she was staying elsewhere).

Next, another friend recommended the Unitarian church as alternative. Following a church picnic where I met members of the congregation, I began receiving letters from a man in a church leadership position who avowed interest in me. He said his wife and he had an open marriage.

He showed me photos of my daughter and me that he'd taken at that picnic. His calls became more frequent. On one occasion of my being sick, he offered to bring me chicken soup, and during that call, he offered to take more photos of my daughter, as she played with her toys...ate a meal... took a bath "au naturel."

At that, I froze. I believed him a predator.

Following that, I returned to the Catholic church, thinking "Better the Devil I know."

Six years later, I married my second husband, a man who belonged to no church. Because I was a divorced Catholic, we were married by a Justice of the Peace. And we began going to an alternative Catholic church whose membership comprised those who wanted more laity involvement with their church.

But this marriage, too, was fraught with abuse. In desperation, I sought a referral from our Pastor who recommended a professional therapist in our church. That man's unprofessional behavior (he invited us to parties at his house and flew ultralight planes with my husband, for sport), kept me in that abusive relationship for the next many years. He never assigned responsibility to my husband for controlling his rage; moreover, he enabled my husband, saying in response to each violent episode I described, "Now, Car-leen (there's no r in my name), what did you do to provoke him?"

When my husband was diagnosed with terminal cancer, I'd find out how dangerous faulty therapy can be.

Before my husband's third chemo round, in an unprovoked rage, he attacked me, violently. We separated after that. The therapist apologized to me for the many times he dismissed my concerns...even offered to provide a room to my husband in his home (my husband refused).

After a separation of several months, I allowed my husband back in our home, when I thought he was at the final stage...but only when my parents agreed to live with us.

It would be another grueling year before he died...but not before inflicting long-term trauma on us, his family.

Despite everything, I kept going to my church.

Two years later, I met a man who was a Catholic widower. We went together for two years, became engaged, and since we were both Catholics, I began the annulment process for marriage #1 which I was told would come easily enough. (He wanted to marry via a Justice of the Peace, in the meantime, but I thought that ceremony superfluous, requiring too much paperwork regarding past unions.)

Since we planned the wedding for the summer, I signed my younger daughter up for a month-long camp stay in Maine, near my sister's home, so my soon-to-be husband and I could enjoy a European honeymoon.

We put our homes on the market, packed or sold household items, bought a new home and financed it together, based on our combined income.

But my fiancée died....two weeks after we moved in....and before we were married.

That reality plunged me into another dark chapter of my life.

The annulment arrived when I no longer needed it– in late November.

I appealed to my local Catholic church to help me find a woman to watch my daughter, from 7:00-8:30 A.M. every day, the time period my new husband was supposed to oversee, when I went off to teach. But I never heard.

It was the local Baptist minister who found the woman who'd fill that need for the next few years.

In the meantime, I took my daughter to that Catholic church in our new neighborhood. She was confirmed there; she played for many church sports teams, while I joined the choir and began writing of church events for the local newspaper.

An argument with our less-than-appreciative Pastor ended my doing that work.

And when my daughter went away to a university in Canada, I ceased going to church.

In our fifth year in North Carolina, I tried once again to connect with my religion. Paul and I began going to St. Eugene's in Woodfin, where I joined the adult choir. But I complained to Paul that the young choir director failed to provide me with the music sheets and never bothered to introduce me to the group.

At first, I excused his omission on the fact I'd signed on during the busy season of Lent and thought him preoccupied, directing the children's choir and instrumentalists.

Then my spiritual world was rocked, in one final blow.

The choir director/music minister, Paul Lawrence Berrell, 28 years old, was charged with sexual exploitation of a minor, one of his students, at his apartment. "Berrell coerced a 13-year-old girl to engage in sexually explicit conduct for the purpose of producing a visual depiction of the conduct," court documents state (March, 12, 2010, Asheville Citizens-Times).

Prosecutors and a clergy victims' support group asserted Berrell had a pattern of abuse, in previous assignments in Georgia, Massachusetts, and Tennessee, from 2002 on.

When police arrested him, Berrell called the Pastor to inform him of the charges, and the latter allegedly went to the choir director's home to purge the music minister's computer of hundreds of pictures depicting child pornography.

This violation was the last straw. Over the years, I'd tolerated what I regarded the church's blatant exclusion of single parishioners who never met their dubious standards; they had never been there for me at critical times in my life.

But this abuse of a child, by a person in a position of trust, a person I knew (or thought I knew), personally, pushed me over the line...finally.

What happened to the young music minister? He's currently doing twenty-eight years in a federal prison.

And the Pastor? I have no knowledge of his whereabouts, but he's no longer at St. Eugene's.

And I'm no longer a member of any church.

I Go to Jail

In our first year, in Asheville, I determined, like so many other retired people, to volunteer my services. After all, I was only 61, it was still a too long winter to merely sit around, read, or watch occasional television shows. With that in mind, I wondered: "What could I do to utilize my talent and contribute in a meaningful way?"

Paul had recently retired from his second career as correctional officer, at Rhode Island's Adult Correctional Institution and I thought: "Why not offer my services to incarcerated women in Asheville?" I could teach them writing skills...vocabulary...whatever.

And so, I contacted the Asheville Jail and they advised me that an instructor from a local higher education facility taught English skills to the women. They suggested I align my services with her.

"Jane" (not her real name) and I met and I instantly knew I could work with her. Each week we expounded on the elements of language, bringing our unique talents to women who sorely needed them. But there were problems. We were assigned to teach some fifteen women in an alleged multi-purpose room, an insulated, windowless space that easily encouraged germ exchange. As a person who got frequent colds—and even pneumonia—I was concerned with the physical limitations.

Then we got into real trouble, because of me.

We planned a special treat using audio-visual equipment one night, but when we arrived to teach, I discovered I'd forgotten my clearance pass. So, like any good felon, I talked my way into the facility, and the person on duty let us in. Was it a breach of security? Yes, but the way I saw it: Better this than disappoint our women who had very little to look forward to.

Besides, we were hardly a threat.

The jail officials didn't see it that way. They were incensed that we didn't follow protocol, and they didn't buy my rationale of "Isn't it better this breach occurred with us, so it insures this doesn't happen with one bent on a nefarious plan?"

We were chastened.

But I knew I couldn't keep delivering in the crowded space afforded us. I wanted a classroom. With that in mind, I put in a request for one, during the day, for the following year, but that request was denied.

They said they simply didn't have the personnel to afford me security that would be required to run my program as I wished.

With that, I terminated my service, and I think the jail was just as happy I did.

But my experience at the Asheville Jail spurred on my plan the following summer, in Rhode Island, where I taught women prisoners at the Gloria MacDonald Facility of Rhode Island's Adult Correctional Institute (prison) a ten-week course on all aspects of writing.

To prepare, I attended a day-long workshop the Corrections Department held.

I called my program "Word Warriors;" I developed my own material; made copies, using the prison's copying machines; and I delivered a two-hour session, free, each week. No correctional officers were present at these sessions, where I engaged with my women.

The toughest part for me was getting through the security devices while wearing an underwire bra (the metal detector went off), and I wondered why officials never warned me not to wear such, in that full-day orientation session.

Once in the facility, I had to lug all my teaching materials to the cramped, hot room where I taught my women. It was hardly easy duty.

Why was I so motivated to teach women prisoners, both in Asheville and Rhode Island? I'd been a single parent for much of my life; I'd overcome tough, challenging experiences, but I always realized that a big reason I overcame the odds stacked against me was my education—my ability to support my family.

I also knew that most of the women who got in trouble with the law were abused; they had drug or alcohol problems; they descended in a never-ending spiral of destruction.

I understood that part of their story, too.

If I had never gotten in trouble with the law, I considered myself lucky, for my education enabled me to make a living and support my kids.

I always recognized: Other women are not nearly as fortunate.

I'm an Avatar

It makes sense that one can leap off tree stations in the sky to glide like a bird, in Asheville, for this town is for adventurers of all types.

In James Cameron's "Avatar," the Na'vis of Pandora inhabit an Earth-like moon of the Alpha Centauri star system. They are a pure and superior breed of humanoids who harbor deep respect for the land (you know—like Ashevillians). These ten foot beings have incredible athletic prowess as they leap astride dragons and ride them through the skies. They're true Avatars in every sense.

For a brief time, and after paying $99.00, I was an Avatar. I was anointed such by my guide at the zip-lining reserve, Navitat, in Barnardsville, western North Carolina, following my successful completion of my task: Course along the sky, two hundred feet up, tethered to cables, brake gradually, and alight onto a tree stump fixed to the timber platform some nine hundred feet away, and do it all in one smooth move.

But, it wasn't easy...

First, our little band of eight were brought up the gravel roadway in four-wheel-drive vehicles; we were fitted with harnesses; and we were prepped as to what we could expect, by knowledgeable guides.

By that point, there was no turning back. (Well, there was, but I felt it too humiliating.)

At our first jumping-off station, we watched the group in front of us hurtle through open space, one at a time, flying over steel cables, going from one high timber platform to another. We learned the fine art of canonballing (same one in diving) so as to control torque (sound impressive?).

The sport is called zip-lining. But its legions of supporters are mostly young, athletic types who like to push the envelope. You know, the same ones who navigate past razor-edged rocks in white water rafting or jump out of planes at twenty thousand feet. They live for the thrill.

Most grandmothers of 66 years of age don't partake.

But I did, for I had the supreme misfortune of mentioning zip-lining to my visiting younger daughter, and she wouldn't be dissuaded from trying it. With that, we signed on for the $99.00, three and one half hour tour that saw us leap off eight treehouse-type platforms, rappel two others, and negotiate a rope sky bridge whose planks were waaaayyy too far apart for my comfort. (I could see the ground far below.)

Right off the first platform (I was first of the eight of us), I didn't brake in time and slammed into our guide at the second tree station. From the outset, I'd realigned my skeletal system–and his, too, probably.

Following that, our guide positioned me last, perhaps thinking my performance might kill others' morale. That heightened my anxiety, for now I had to await the flight of all and then I come at them, full-force, akin to a bowling ball, hurtling at the pins.

Few knew my real emotional state. A young woman who was nervous, herself, even accused me of being "wonderfully relaxed, appearing like a pro," while I thought: I really have mastered that adage: "Never let 'em see you sweat."

At periodic points, in the leaping off or rappelling, our guide pointed out flora and fauna, the trees, how the bark "talks" and gives information to help one classify.

I feigned polite interest, but seriously… all I *really* wanted was a transport vehicle akin to sleds used to ferry injured skiers, down slopes, at ski resorts. But there were no such escape mechanisms. I had to finish what I'd signed on for, despite the fact I was exhausted; my limbs shook; I wanted a bathroom; and I was parched in the way only terror effects.

But if you'd seen me course through the trees, you'd have thought I was having the time of my life. I screamed, too. In fact, we all did…we were encouraged to do so, for apparently, screaming's a primal right of those who fly through those air corridors at thirty-five miles per hour, while the ground disappears below.

The difference? My screams were real.

But at the end of a day of zip-lining, I'd become an Avatar, and I can honestly say: I'm thrilled I did it. The frosting on the cake is when my daughter said: "Finn, Sam, and Luke would think you're a pretty cool grandmother for doing this."

And I thought: Sometimes, in life, just looking the part is good enough.

P.S. I vaulted the Asheville sky some years ago; I believe Navitat has made improvements since, such as a new braking system on the cables (probably all owing to me). But I don't know if they ever got those restrooms strategically placed along the route, the ones folks need when they're terrified.

Just sayin.'

The Bells of Beaver Lake, North Asheville

Across from Beaver Lake, in North Asheville, there's a house that sits atop a hill that is covered by vines, and on an eave of that house hang fat steel tubes (wind chimes) that clang deep, resonant sounds.

Much smaller brass chimes hang nearby. They tinkle softly...

Together, they deliver a cacophony of hope, and I admit: I needed it on this dark day.

Ominous thoughts pervaded and I couldn't shake despondency, for I was at a crossroads. Sometimes, life smacks me down and forces me to confront my own reality. It's happened to me before.

I tell Paul I'll jog with him, but I don't really feel like it. My legs are heavy, and I lack commitment. I want very much to wallow in my own misery.

But I don't.

I get out of the car and proceed to walk. He stays with me. A cool wind whips about, and I curse it, at first. Then I realize: It buoys me and refuses the normal order of things which sees my energy sapped in such circumstances. You see, I suffer from a mild case of multiple sclerosis.

With this breeze, however, I feel lighter.

Coming upon two others who walk their dogs along the lake, I say "Hello," and then ask if they know why the lake water has a strange, brownish cast to it. The man tells me that upstream waters feed down, from a construction site on a hill nearby, creating silt-laden waters. Those waters wash toward the lake.

In addition, there'd been a big storm earlier in the week that kicked up the lake's floorbed.

They know the personality of the lake; they've lived in Asheville many years.

Thereupon, we four enter into a lively conversation of some fifteen to twenty minutes. We laugh...we share...we enjoy one another's company and I marvel: If I hadn't gotten out of the car...if I'd given in to my misery...if I couldn't reach out to others, I'd be locked into my own negativity.

We part company, promising to continue a conversation, in future. They're inveterate Beaver Lake Walkers, as are we.

As I continue on the path, now alone (Paul jogs ahead), I stop in my tracks when I hear the deep chimes...then the gentle ones, following, in that order.

I stand, quietly taking it all in.

It's random moments such as these that I feel the deepest spiritual connection.

Perhaps it's no coincidence I discovered (in course of that earlier conversation with the couple), he's a minister of God, and she's that minister's wife. Now, just for the record, I'm not looking to be proselytized, for as I said: I'm a defrocked Catholic who's now an agnostic or maybe even an atheist (except that means 'belief' in no god, and as I said the belief part eludes me right now).

No matter. I secretly thank them for helping me break out of a dark place. You see, I'll take my golden moments wherever I can get them.

Now, have you ever been pulled out of a deep hole of despair by a seemingly irrelevant event, then thought later: "If that hadn't happened, I'd still be rooted in negativity?"

Agents of change are all about: Interesting people...nature's beauty...wind chimes on a house...Or a combination of the above...

Now, my question: Are they ever really random?

Stately sycamore trees' first cousin, the London Plane trees, with their knobby bark, stand sentry along Merrimon Ave., while a dog sits sentry, awaiting his master, at Beaver Lake, Woodfin, NC.

Asheville and Surrounds: Land of Contradictions

Gunrunners' pic of AK-47 on one end of this building vies with "Jesus Is Lord" on the other. Seeming contradiction? This building's in Tennessee, a short distance from the North Carolina border.

Asheville's a friendly little place….A sweet haven in an eclectic pot.

Interesting boutiques and bistros dot the cityscape. But a short way out of Asheville, one sees gun emporiums and Confederate flags. And those flags aren't "flying second," as they're supposed to, deferring to the higher American flag on the pole.

Rather, that Southern flag flying solo confirms the fact that the owner is in oppositional mode to the government or still rooted in a Civil War mentality. In any case, one does notice.

I've often said Asheville's "the Land of Older Hippies." In response to my own question, some years back of "Who settles here?" I determined: Hippies with a little (or a lot of) money. Or the next generation of "Greeners" (those concerned with the environment), the "Anti-Any-War Faction" or "Folks Against Corporate America."

Paul and I are probably in the first group, but we made our lifetime money in the very industries some of us criticized.

You see, once we discovered that communal farms often fail (because everyone doesn't share the same work ethic), we took jobs in corporate America, or entered its corollary–the service industries–in order to support our families. We exchanged our Beetle Volkswagens for family vans and began living in the suburbs of America.

Little League, scouting, sports events, and dance lessons took our focus. We were ever-more-involved in our kids' activities.

But now, when that phase is over, those of us who are lucky to have health and enough financial stability to make choices, find ourselves strangely drawn (is it serendipity?) to a unique enclave of the world...Asheville.

And Asheville is unique.

When people ask: "What's it like?" I tell them honestly, "Like nothing or nowhere you've ever been before." I mean, "How many times do you go food shopping and hear minstrels strumming guitars, right outside the doors. Or therapists giving folks on-the-spot neck massages, while shoppers walk about?"

But Asheville's not for everyone.

Oh, it's got its oddities, too. I can't count the times Paul and I have gone for a ride in outlying countryside, only to discover "Dead End" after going down the road for fifteen miles! (My GPS isn't always reliable.) And forget cell phone use. There are no towers in outlying regions.

And never be misled by the suffix "Cove" on road signs, such as Tunnel Cove Road. My first year, (homesick as I was for the ocean), I went barreling down such a road, hoping to find fresh water ponds and lakes. That never happened. "Cove" in western North Carolina, according to natives, allegedly means "safe harbor," metaphorically. Or more specifically, "between the mountains." Cove refers to a land mass, not water.

What about the "liberal" label? Well, that depends on who's asking. Folks here are liberal about what they're liberal about. For instance, there's probably a heavy contingent that's anti-gun (they're the former Peacenik activists or children of same). But they're probably not averse to using violence to enforce their pacifist position.

Strangely enough, and because Asheville's "All About Rights," the pacifists live shoulder-to-shoulder with guardians of their Second Amendment rights, the gun people. In short, that means: The latter group loudly and openly defend their right to have (and carry) guns.

Then, there are the super-religious types, spouting Christ's message. Crosses appear (some vying with the giant Christ statue, looking over Rio de Janeiro, in Brazil), on hillsides, reminding all that Jesus's blood was spilled, for the redemption of mankind. One doesn't get the idea, however, that they'd be terribly tolerant of other religions they consider foreign and anti-American.

That message on a hillside is often spelled out–graphically.

Vegans, another no-nonsense group, can become carnivorous when it comes to their combative feeling about meat-eaters, though, and if folks sport fur, watch out! The fur flies.

Mostly, Asheville's just waaayyy different from anywhere else. There are many older Americans there who are unique in the fact they embrace their years as a badge of honor.

Many senior folks, here, launch second or third careers, too, for they've still got entrepreneurial spirit. Or maybe their previous careers didn't get them where they want to be.

But most are knowledgeable about current issues and vocal as to what they support and reject.

Even if they still wear their Birkenstocks (in some instances, they're the same ones they had in the 60's).

Part III: What You Might *Not* Like About the Region

Weekends Are Different There

I loved the Countess's line in "Downton Abbey:" "What's a weekend?" in response to a dinner guest who referred to the days following a full work week that most working folks enjoy. Why didn't she know the term? As member of the gentry class, she wouldn't understand the concept, for every day is a weekend day to those who don't have to work for a living.

In the Northeast and regions other than the Bible Belt, the weekend, for most, is a time for relaxation and cutting loose. But retail shops are open, in recognition of the fact that the public has leisure time to shop.

That's not the case in much of the South and this fact takes serious adjusting by newcomers moving into the region who are used to businesses accommodating to the public all the time.

After all, the South's not called the "Bible Belt" for nothing. It's a swath of territory comprised of Arkansas, Mississippi, Alabama, Tennessee, Georgia, South Carolina, Kentucky, and usually North Carolina, states deeply rooted in Protestant (mostly Baptist) belief. As a result, little white churches dot the countryside (almost as many as Starbucks cafes in Seattle, the birthplace for that city's ubiquitous brand), and huge stone edifices dedicated to distinct Protestant sects, proliferate the more urban Southern realms.

On Sundays, following services, families of the faithful come streaming in to Applebee's, Cracker Barrel's, Ruby Tuesday's, with men wearing suits and girls and women fancy-dressed, as well. To us northerners, it's like we've stepped back in time, to the 1950's era.

One overhears sweet tea, ordered, again and again—as beverage of choice. In the Bible Belt, beer, wine, and other mixed drinks are the exception—not the rule.

Church isn't just for Sundays, either. On Wednesday, Baptists revisit the religious scene, where they get reminded, mid-week, of God's laws and how they can comply.

So, it's church service on Sunday morning, come back for refresher course in evening, and then midweek, on Wednesday.

Think they don't get their crowds? Think again. On one Superbowl Sunday, when I traveled along Rt. 40 to Asheville, coming from the airport, following a New Jersey visit, I passed church after church whose lights bathed the landscape. I was stunned, thinking: "My God, they even swell the church pews on this most sacred day of football."

I don't believe this Catholic girl ever saw such devotion in New England—even during Lent.

And because it's the Bible Belt, businesses operating in the usual sense (24/7) is anything but the norm. After all, the South is the region from which Chick fil-A emanated. And in true "practice what you preach," their company policy dictates they close on Sunday, the Lord's day of rest.

If you need a professional, such as a dentist, you may just have to wait until the work week, as I sadly found out when I cracked my tooth on a cherry pit one Friday evening. I called approximately twenty dentist offices, all of whom had recordings, but none responded. When I left Asheville, a few years later, however, I did

160

note one dentist touting weekend availability, smartly hoping to tap into that market.

But hair stylist closed for the weekend was, to me, a real stunner, for back in New England, weekends are generally a stylist's busiest.

Just another "opposite" to which one must adjust in the South.

Here's a typical little church, right outside Canton, North Carolina, the paper mill town, devoid of all superfluous fuss, in keeping with Baptist belief.

In the region, you'll see a lot of little white churches like this one, just outside downtown Canton.

Snow Is Serious in the South

My first winter in Asheville, I was smug indeed. I recall the afternoon, particularly. I was at the Asheville Mall, on Tunnel Road, when a TV weather advisory came over the PA system, warning that the region could expect some snow. The Malls were empty of all but a few stalwart types. I chuckled inwardly at the temerity of these Southern inhabitants: "What were they afraid of?" "My God, the forecast was for a dusting."

Two hours later, with purchases in hand, I cleared the inch or two from my car windows and proceeded to travel the nine-plus miles to Weaverville, north of downtown. Since I thought the highway might be more heavily trafficked, with big rigs, I stuck to the alternate, in-town route, Merrimon Ave.

When I got to the Beaver Lake region, the driving got tough. Three to four inches of heavy snow was on a roadway that hadn't been cleared or treated in any way—not with salt or sand. In my SUV, I gingerly crept forward, fearful that I'd go off the road or worse yet, get behind some timid soul that believed the way to drive in snowy conditions was to inch along...even up inclines.

I saw a few cars with chains on their tires, a throwback to an earlier era, and I marveled: "Wow, I haven't seen that since I was a girl!" I couldn't imagine why they'd be necessary but then again: I hadn't thought through the fact all those mountainous roads defy mere salting and plowing. Chains were apparently the only way to go.

Then it happened. On the last leg of my journey, on Reems Creek Road, I came upon a truck cresting the hill, whose wheels were spinning. If I continued on my course, I knew I'd be adversely affected by the truck's inability to make the ascent, either stuck behind him or forced to pass, blindly, on the hill of a two-lane road. At 6:00 P.M., it was already pitch black and I had no real idea who might be coming up the hill from the opposite direction– just a hope I'd be able to detect him, in advance, by oncoming headlights—if the driver had them on.

I sucked in my breath and accelerated, shaking violently as I considered the risk. The tires of my SUV spun but caught intermittently, and I zig-zagged my way to the top, barely avoiding the truck who was now stuck, mid-hill. I crested and limped down the other side, my stomach churning, all the while. .

When I got home, I almost kissed the white-blanketed ground.

Later on, in the townhome complex, we lost electricity, due to the storm. This caused another volley of insanity as I attempted to report the outage to the electric company. Me: "Hello, we've lost power at Hamburg Crossing." "You say, Ma'am, you're at a hamburger place?" the responder answered. "No, I'm calling about a power outage at Hamburg Crossing, the townhome community in Weaverville, on Reems Creek Road."

Now, I knew why folks in this region never go out when bad weather is forecast but wisely wait until the snow melts and all returns to normalcy. No use for municipalities to pay significant outlay of funds for salt and sand when Mother Nature takes care of the problem, expeditiously, when the temperatures rise above freezing almost the very next day.

Like everything else in the South, if one is just patient, the problem will resolve itself.

In future, if meteorologists forecast snow, I delayed an excursion.

Except in the case of a friend's colonoscopy.

I'd promised Susan I'd take her for this difficult procedure. The poor thing had already had one failed attempt the month before, and since I'm a veteran of this procedure, I wanted no new problems to scuttle her second try.

I looked out the morning of her appointment day to see heavy snow accumulating and a car ditched in the drainage moat aside our community. I wondered: "Should I call and tell her I couldn't possibly drive in these conditions?" I wondered, too, if the medical facility had closed for the day.

Then I considered all the people who would've completed the preparation and knew they'd never close the facility short of the doctor's demise. When Paul offered to drive us, I jumped at the chance and promised to take him to breakfast, as a treat.

With that, we set off, picked up Susan, and arrived at the doctor's office.

While there, our friend filled out the appropriate paperwork and the clerk at the reception desk informed us that we'd need to wait...we couldn't go off, about our business, as was our custom, back in our home state, whenever one of us had this procedure.

In Asheville, this gastroenterologist required the party who brought the patient to remain in the waiting room, throughout the procedure, in a sort of share-the-punishment routine.

So, that day, when the storm swirled outside and our friend had a colonoscopy that checked her internal workings, we sat, hungry and impatient in the waiting room, reading every magazine in sight.

Just another Asheville quirk.

Oh, we did go out to eat after. Our friend treated us to what was now a very late lunch, during which time the restaurant waitress told us a garbage truck had careened off the road we'd traveled earlier, tying up traffic on Merrimon Ave. for hours.

In future, I asked girlfriends to avoid making colonoscopy appointments when seasonal complications could make a difficult procedure all the more abysmal.

But that incident taught me never to dismiss the almost-daily, in-winter reports of snow and ice for the region. Schools and businesses are shut down, or delayed, since mountain roads are impossible to keep clear (snow and ice melts on the sun side, only to freeze again, later), and snowfall can be significantly different even a mile or two down the road, depending on vectors, shifts in altitude, etc.

Those experiences taught this New England girl a respect for winter weather in the mountains of North Carolina.

In future, I wasn't so quick to chuckle at "snow chickens" who kept off the roads lest they invite disaster.

Doctors Not Easily Accessible for Two-State Folks

Business magazines rate retirement communities on a host of issues that retired people deem important: Climate, cost of living, recreational and social opportunities, medical availability are all factors people consider. Retired people want their doctors to be highly accessible and excellent.

But that criterion is hard to meet for part-time residents of Asheville, and I wonder if that's a similar problem in other geographic locations to which retirees flock.

I've gotta admit: medical services were a big reason for our moving to Asheville, North Carolina. Since I'm a breast cancer survivor, I deemed it important to choose a town that got high marks for its medical facilities and providers. I wanted my primary provider and specialists there plentiful and professional. I already had all of those in place, in my home state.

But Asheville is a town where the ranks of older Americans swell, due to so many retirees arriving.

I was fortunate. In that first year, a friend recommended Dr. Michael Messino, an oncologist at Western North Carolina Cancer Center, and I continued going to him for the entire time we lived in Asheville.

A sensitive, caring man, Dr. Messino hugs his patients, upon greeting, or warmly takes their hands, a trait I found both endearing and refreshing. I determined, early on, that if I had to receive another round of bad news (such as reoccurrence of cancer), I'd want him to deliver it.

Fortunately, he never needed to. But he did refer me to surgeons on two occasions, when concerns following mammograms warranted. In the nine years I was in Asheville, I had two out-patient, surgical procedures. In both instances, I had the services of top surgeons.

For that's also what Dr. Messino provided: He became a referral source for me, since I was new to the region. When I needed a primary care provider, he gave me Dr. James Hoer's name, and I must say: I was pleased there, too, for Hoer's office provides a walk-in clinic for their patients who seek immediate treatment of non-critical problems (like colds) or professional assessment by a Physician Assistant who determines if one's problem requires more serious attention.

Dr. Messino provided me with a dentist's name, too– the person he goes to. And finally, he gave me the podiatrist who put an end to persistent pain in my foot.

I'd tried, unsuccessfully, to get the medical attention I wanted elsewhere. I'd gone to an Asheville orthopedic center in the past, for another problem, and when a new and particularly painful problem with a nerve, presented in my foot, I sought their orthopedic services. I had to wait six weeks for my appointment and when I finally got in, the doctor told me he "didn't give cortisone shots."

This greatly disturbed me, since, when I'd made the appointment, I specifically asked if I could get that cortisone shot, a treatment my Rhode Island podiatrist had recommended. The Rhode

Island doctor had advised I make the appointment as soon as I arrived in Asheville, in January, realizing I might have trouble getting in with a specialist immediately.

As it was, I didn't get help with my problem until we were set to go back home, five months later. In desperation, I called Dr. Messino's office again, with a request for a podiatrist name.

What happened? By mentioning my oncologist's name as referral source, I got the appointment within two weeks, and the podiatrist gave me the cortisone shot. Now, six months out, I am still pain-free.

But this getting in to see specialists was not just a problem in this instance. Some years back, I had difficulty getting in to see a dermatologist, too. Oh, I could see the physician assistant earlier, but it would be five months out, if I wanted to see the dermatologist, as "new patient."

Since I'm a person who's had melanoma, I consider seeing the doctor, quickly, essential to my well-being.

All this tells me one thing: There aren't enough providers of medical services for the ever-escalating population in Asheville. The situation for two-state residents is so dire that they may want to follow the advice I offered in my column "Asheville Under Glass," appearing in western North Carolina's newspaper, *Mountain Xpress:*

"Get Your Docs (Not 'Ducks') Lined Up"

Where is that Obamacare medical warehouse we all were promised? You know, the one that will store our medical data such as the list of meds we take, when we had our last tetanus shot, operation dates, etc. I, for one, will embrace a Big Brother information-gathering site, for I want aspects of my health housed in one area, so my life is easier.

Here's how one problem developed, when I tried to make an appointment with a dermatologist:

(Me, with decided urgency)..."Hi...I'm Colleen Mellor and I'm a half-year resident of Asheville who also lives in Rhode Island. I have this particularly pesky problem with a cyst that's worrisome. I'm an established patient who came in a while ago (I'm purposely vague)...I believe I'm in your computer system...

I hear paper shuffling and computer clicking during which time the receptionist locates my information and asks me questions. I confirm my birthdate and address, and I'm heartened, for she's found proof I'm an established patient. Then she says: "Hmmmm. ...I'm sorry but since you've not been here, in quite some time, you've been discontinued as "Active Patient." You'll now need to make an appointment as "New Patient."

Because I don't really recognize the import of this, I say "Oh, that's OK....So when can I get an appointment as 'New Patient'?"

(She says, apologetically...) The doctor isn't taking "New Patients" until June (I called in March), so that would be the earliest.

(Me, incredulously): "June? Are you serious? (that's rhetorical). If this is an infection, I'll be dead by then." (Now, on second thought, I rethink what I say and offer): "Ooooh, wait a minute... I think there's supposed to be a big snowstorm coming in, mid-week, and I'm sure some North Carolinian will cancel his or her appointment when roads get slick. Can you put me on a waiting list to get me in when someone cancels? I then add (in a wild effort to bond with this woman) that we Northeasterners drive though anything." She laughs but then gets serious...

Well...I can't put you in just anyone's canceled slot. You can only take a New Patient's canceled appointment...

(Me, getting flustered): "But I'm not really a New Patient, because I've been to the doctor before, and it's not my fault the computer reclassifed me. I just haven't had a dermatological problem in the past four years, so I had no reason to come" (at this point,

I'm sure the infection is that flesh-eating bacteria we've all read about).

"What do you suggest I do?" I ask, in shrouded panic.

"Well, are you willing to see the PA (physician assistant)?"

I get excited and say "Yes," but then she tells me the PA's next available appointment is in May.

But, she adds: if you take that May appointment, it'll get you in the door. In the meantime, I suggest you go to your general practitioner so he can check out your problem. He can put you on antibiotics, too, if need."

Now, for the record, my general practitioner in Asheville had to be cajoled into seeing me last year when I got a cold and needed medication because it'd been a couple of years since I saw him, also. His computer also dropped me from "Active Patient" status.

You see, I have my yearly check-up with my primary care provider, Dr. Chad Lamendola, in Rhode Island and Medicare has rules for paying for more than one annual physical, so I hadn't seen my Asheville primary care provider, Dr. Hoer, for quite some time either.

As a follow-up: I went to Dr. Hoer's walk-in clinic for established patients where Physician Assistant, Kathy Haggart, treated me. I'm thrilled: Seems I don't have that flesh-eating bacteria after all...

She got me an appointment with a surgeon for the following Monday (she has clout).

And she got me in to see that same dermatologist I wanted, in two weeks (more clout).

My advice? Get your docs lined up before you need them, and if you're a two-state resident, send all test results, procedures, medication lists to all, so you never get de-activated.

You might also want to have periodic wellness check appointments...not for you... but for your doctors. For instance, I see my oncologist, Dr. Michael Messino, of Asheville, yearly, to assure myself that *he's* fine.

I don't plan on being "deactivated" ever again. It's just too damned hard to get resuscitated.

Here's pic of Paul, snoozing behind his germ-retardant mask, as he accompanies me to that walk-in clinic, on Biltmore Ave., where the Well Waiting Room separates the Sick Room, but one must be an established Dr. Hoer patient to access this clinic. They'll get you into the specialists you need, as well.

Asheville Woman Looking for a Man? "Good Luck!"

I tell him all the time: "If something happens to me (as in "death"), there'll be a line, ten layers deep, encircling our townhome, comprised of women anxious to take my place." I go on: "They'll come unbidden, with casserole dishes, or some similar lure, to ensnare you (my unsuspecting partner)."

And I told him he'd comply, if only to assuage his loneliness and a hollow belly.

After all, he lives in the male-centric universe that proves he's a hot item—at any age. And that rule is all the more applicable in Asheville.

For one thing, my guy's a proven entity: physically fit, tolerably fine personality, occasionally funny or witty. He has a sort of oblique charm and an unflappable ability to fix things. In short, he's the answer to any woman's prayer.

He's cute, too, in a dimple-in-his-cheek, irreverent sort of way, weighing in at the same one hundred and seventy-six pounds he's carried most of his life. How does he keep his athletic build? He's got a strange metabolism that acts as if it's 18 years old, allowing him to eat anything with few dire consequences.

And he's physically active (he was a 5k jogger until some years back, following the accident), but he continues to do perpetual yard clean-up and swimming pool maintenance on a daily basis. He's anything but lazy.

Finally, a twenty-five year relationship with me, a successful woman, has cemented his stance.

He's got other virtues as well, the kind that become increasingly important with age.

The fact he had three careers (trucking, corrections, and National Guard) means he gets three pensions, and when one is older, pensions and benefits are paramount. Attractiveness is no longer merely about a taut physique or handsome face.

And because he was career military, he gets medical benefits through TriCare. All this bumps him way up on the Mate Meter, for he's one of a select minority, an endangered species, if you will.

But most people don't know about his tangible, financial perks. They do, however, still notice his appearance.

I recall grocery shopping at the upscale local grocery store, Fresh Market, in Asheville, recently, where a little old woman of 80 years stood before me in line. I'd become exasperated because I thought Paul (with lightly filled shopping basket) was right behind me, but due to his attention deficit disorder that sees him distracted by any new product put in a shopper's visual field, he allowed two other women with bulging carriages to intervene in the line, right behind me.

He never recalls my admonition that women will jump the line, if they can, recognizing the grocery store as turf-war-territory. Men never know that, and even if they've been told, they quickly forget.

When he sidestepped them to come behind me, I apologized to all for his putting us in this awkward position. That's when the little old lady in front of me turned and reproached me with "You better be nice to him...He's cute. A lot of us would take him off your hands."

Resenting her nerviness, I countered: "So, you think it would be that easy...do you?"

But her words got me to thinking. Even dawdling, absent-mindedly, in a grocery store, my older, male partner becomes a prize worthy of competition.

One of the husbands in our townhome complex recently decried the growing preponderance of single older women, in our community, as if the women were personally responsible for mates' predeceasing them.

I think, more than anything, he feared the proverbial handwriting on the wall that said he might be next. Maybe his wife would then join other widows in walking loops about the complex, new pets in tow, widows who seemed content enough.

But if I didn't see the ratio inequity played out before me, in our complex, I have only to look to girlfriends who bemoan the shortage of appropriate male partners for trips, gatherings, social events, dinners, conversation, or even an occasional sexual fling. These all tell me Asheville's not spawning ground for heterosexual pairing.

Unless one's male, for in this lopsided universe, they don't even need to seek; women will pile up at their doorstep.

Conversely, gays of both types (male to male and female to female) or swing-hitters, are eminently more suited to partnership in this mountain enclave.

Who's the loneliest tribe? Single women seeking men.

Got a good man in Asheville? Watch other women who might just be circling around like buzzards, waiting for you to croak.

As Jack Webb, of "Dragnet" would say: (These are) "just the facts, ma'am."

Bad Boys in Trucks

They're unnerving as they sweep through town in the darkening hours, with giant Confederate flags, fluttering in the wind, pegged to the flatbed part of their trucks. I can almost hear the racist chant that might accompany their nighttime rides and probably does burst forth, on occasion.

They are the odd contrast in a region that got its swelling population from the surge of incomers who were former Peacenik activists, my heretofore anointed "hippies with money," for in Asheville and immediate areas, liberalism abounds. It stands in stark contrast to others who are most probably native to the region.

For these are the bad boys who live in the fringe areas, the ones who hang those same giant flags across doorways of their trailers, signifying to all that they pay homage first to another mindset that signifies to most Northerners—repression and a system that glorified the enslavement of others.

Or they position those same gigantic Confederate flags on the highest hill of their many-acre property, shouting their opposition to the government.

They have that same flag symbol tacked to their license plates, too, or prominently displayed on back windows of their vehicles, the same window that showcases their shotgun poised across the glass expanse, in its interior holder.

Often, these men live in compounds of several trailers, a sort of militia training ground, where men of all ages, stand sentry duty or walk about, armed with rifles.

These are all most probably the folks at odds with what's happened in our country in recent years, with its demographic changes and influx of other ethnic groups, yellow, brown or black--decidedly not white.

These are the ranks of angry white voters so powerful in our last election—the disenfranchised who have been left out, when other groups gained economic ground.

Their fury is understandable—if frightening. Their towns have folded up, with a minority eking out a living as businesses died and their young had to go elsewhere, for employment. Towns that used to bustle are a shadow of their former selves.

If their jobs were pegged to a certain industry—like furniture-making—they disappeared, gone instead to cheaper production factories in China. The transportation side, too, the railroads that delivered those goods, also took a serious hit, their pallets stand empty and forlorn, their wood rotting.

Now, these former workers are understandably angry.

Many was the time, I wondered (on trips outside the immediate area of Asheville): "How do these folks make a living?" as we passed countless communities outside the commerce centers that appeared anything but on the way up.

Some few have reinvented themselves via the tourist trade, relying on the region's natural beauty and considerable artistic talent, but they are the exception, while many other former bustling towns languish, wondering how they'll compete in this new world, while resenting a new order they don't understand.

And so they ride...at night...and often through darkened streets, their war cry a chilling reminder of what happens when fear rules, for these are the very ones who doubtless fought in our wars, made the sacrifices, and believed in a system they now feel betrayed them.

Kudzu

The science fiction/horror film hit the screen, when I was 13 years of age, and its effects stay with me, even today. Directed by Irvin Yeaworth and starring Steve McQueen, the movie "The Blob" was about an extra-terrestrial life form that came down to earth and swallowed all within its sphere. In the process, it grew to monstrous proportions.

One of the most prescient memories, to me, is when it took over a manufacturing plant, meandering through giant pipes, overcoming all in its path.

But when I saw kudzu for the first time, hanging over lamp posts and power lines along highways threading through the region, I have to say: It gave me pause, for kudzu reminds me of "The Blob." In Southern regions, it appears to grow unabated, and loops over power lines, bushes, fences, telephone poles, blanketing them like some strange alien force that threatens to squeeze out the breath and life from all earthly matter.

And its name is equally strange, like an Asian fighter—Kudzu.

The kudzu vine did not grow naturally in our country. Native to China and Japan, kudzu was introduced to the United States in 1876 during the Centennial Exposition, held in Philadelphia to celebrate the nation's 100th birthday.

For the occasion, the Japanese government created a beautiful garden exhibit, replete with native Japanese plants, including kudzu. Unaware of its potential as an invasive plant, American gardeners soon began to grow kudzu for its attractive, glossy foliage and heavily-scented blossoms similar to wisteria.

In later years, it became popular as feed for cattle and goats. The only problem? Its invasive proliferation, for soon after its introduction, kudzu suffocates all other growth. And that is because the plant has no natural enemies in the United States (bugs that keep it in check), as it does in its homeland. The vine that puts out feelers grows unchecked where there is sunlight and temperate conditions.

Its proliferation in Southern parts shows why there are environmental rules about bringing plant or animal life into regions without approval, in that such life forms can overpopulate and take over, thus changing the eco-systems, by virtue of the fact they have no natural predators.

After all, they weren't supposed to be there, in the original plan. They were trucked in or imported, accidentally, or without regard to long-term effects.

Consider, for instance, the problem of carp in certain areas of the Great Lakes. It is now feared that this particular fish will destroy the marine eco-system by killing off the rest of the aquatic population and preying on smaller fish.

That's what has happened regarding Kudzu. Somehow it was introduced and now it covers significant swaths of the South, giving the region a Disney-like "Forgotten Forest" appearance.

In fact, it got such a negative reputation, some call it "the plant that ate the South."

But seriously, most environmentalists caution that since kudzu needs sunlight to populate, the only real affected areas are the fringe of the forested regions. In other words, kudzu doesn't go deep. It really won't strangle the region and all its inhabitants.

The picture below is of a house on a highway into Greenville, South Carolina, where kudzu appears to have swallowed an entire property—grass...fields...trees....and house.

Part IV: What You'll *Like* About the Region

Craigslist Respondents
Are Colorful There

I'd just posted an Asheville, North Carolina Craigslist ad to sell a '99 Volkswagen Cabrio and the crush of responses began: "Oh, I've been waiting for this kind of car forever," "Can I come to see it now?" The ones who'd lose out were the obvious: "Oh, I love that car, but I've got only $1200...Will you accept that?" (asked probably by a 16 year old). I fought back the sarcastic response: "Now, why would I do that?"

Then there was the woman who wanted me to send her detailed photos of the engine, while I thought: "Yeah, that's not going to happen (while I handle the flood of interest). The car's sixteen years old; the engine reflects that reality."

The sale of this car became a feeding frenzy, one I hardly anticipated.

I responded to the first twenty e-mailers and left messages on others' cell phones. On my last call, a man answered and said his wife "was on the way over to my house to see the car" (they apparently live in the same town). At that, I learned my address was posted along with the ad. (I wrongly thought my stating of our address on the Craigslist question sheet was only for Craigslist internal use.)

I saw her, as she shot across the corner of my lawn, running over the wooden stake, painted bright crimson that Paul planted bolt upright, to remind me not to cut too close to the corner. She pulled in, behind our other car, and left her car's engine running as if she were poised for a quick get-away.

When I said "Woah, you're fast, but I gotta say: There are about twenty other people interested in this car," she replied: "I don't give a shit...I'm here first and I got the money" (she waved a wad of bills up in the air).

I countered with "Now, hold on. You're not necessarily getting the car, since we haven't agreed, and furthermore, if my car's going to you, I'd like *to like you* a little bit (it seems I need this ingredient for anything I sell). Right now, I'm just not sure."

If the truth be told, I feared she'd be the type to come after me, with a Blunderbuss shotgun, if something went wrong with the car.

We talked price. She asked if I'd take lower (all buyers do that), and I reminded her about the interest. She said she'd have to go back home to get the remaining hundreds, from her husband. Since I didn't want her running over a small child in her zeal and because I wondered if she were making the currency on the fly, I went with her.

On the way, we talked about the possibility of needing a notary public, for the title exchange, none of whom I knew.

Susan offered she knew one. We'd go to her, once she retrieved the money.

Kicking away discarded cigarette packs and plastic Orange Crush bottles that had bottle-necked on the floor, I took a seat in her Dodge Dart. The car smelled of stale cigarette smoke, probably owing to the styrofoam cup in the cup holder, containing old butts, floating in yellow-brown water. I considered what my poor car was in for, if she became the new owner. But as a former smoker, myself, I wasn't going to cop a smug attitude.

We traveled over back roads that cut through hills, made a hurried stop at her house, and pushed on to the notary's.

Once there, Susan got out and went to the porch where she rang the bell. In a few moments, a shirtless man came to the door; they talked; and he leaned out, to look at me. When Susan returned to the car to get me, I said "I'm not going in, if he's naked." She chuckled and assured me that though shirtless, he was dressed.

At the door, Susan had a hushed exchange with notary Jennie Mae who avoided my eyes. I wondered if Susan hadn't said, upon entering: "Look, I know she's Northern (my accent always gives me away), but she's got a car I want, so can we get this done?"

I interjected: "Hello Miss Jennie (I've heard Southerners like this formality), I'm Colleen Mellor." I was wrong: Jennie didn't like this. She effected a bored look of "Why'd you feel the need to do that?" about her.

For the next ten minutes, I sat, mutely, as the two women scoured the title form and discussed why a notary's signature probably wasn't necessary. A big clue was that there was no space on the title for a stamp or signature. When they pored over the document, for the third time, Jennie Mae determined to double-check with husband Verne (the aforesaid shirtless one who actually had shorts on the lower half of his anatomy), because Verne's a notary, too. He sat in the next room, in an upholstered strat-o-lounger, smoking cigarettes, and watching TV.

Verne, the final arbiter, said: "No...Notary signature's not necessary."

With that, he took himself out to the side yard to feed the considerable flock of turkeys that had mustered, in the meantime, saying "Time to feed the critters." These wild birds apparently came every day, to his yard, at this time.

Susan and I got back in her car which she steered gingerly through the flock, evidencing far greater caution than she'd ever employed at my property.

And I considered: Craigslist was the culprit who brought together two of us women from very different worlds....Craigslist and the love of a little '99 VW Cabrio that apparently everyone else in western North Carolina loves, too.

Because of our success in selling our car, I then proceeded to list several other items on Craigslist, but none of the other sales rose to the level of "colorful" the car sale provided.

Below is the Northern car that generated so much love and even caused folks to cross usual geographic barriers–our little Volkswagen Cabrio.

Asheville Crafts Are Real Art

It's a staple here, in our region, the Weaverville Art Safari, that is. It's when artists of every stripe open their homes and studios to the public. And I gotta admit: We (of the public) almost always love it, for the variety of people we meet.

But I have to say: Some artists are lucky they sell on the web—or through stores—because they have terrible people skills. In fact, take the "s" off that last word, for some are devoid of any. Instead, they occupy a narcissistic world where they're front and center.

Everyone else is pure backdrop.

Case in point: A jewelry artist we met. Paul and I came through a torturously winding road to get to her home, tacked onto the side of a cliff, only to find her less-than-hospitable. She designs work from clay, bakes it, paints it (and marks it with a "T").

OK, last part isn't necessary or applicable, but I decided to have a little fun. Because I wasn't getting any from her.

Our little visit was "all about her," how she got "too successful," how she's "had to hire so-o many people."

Hers was an "embarrassment of riches," but one where she denied anyone else's value.

Conspicuously absent was her asking us (or others who'd stumbled in) anything about our lives (we were pretty much all of retirement age). She simply had no interest.

So, I decided: I'm not wearing her plumage (jewelry). She's got enough of that going on, in her own head. She represents a batch of artists who've never accomplished the art of the deal.

And I contrast her with an artist cut from a whole different cloth...Asheville's Leo Monahan.

He works in a different medium—paper, and makes sculptures and three-dimensional wall art, both white (as with his owl and bird collection) and those utilizing high-drama, full palette of vibrant hues in his boats, feathers, animals.

Last I saw he was tackling cicadas.

But the man is wonderfully versed in humanity and multi-dimensional, for he truly cares about others.

My meeting him was serendipitous. A friend of mine was doing public relations work for this wonderful artist; she'd spoken of him, but not being a full-time resident, I didn't recognize his name.

She had sent me the link to his website, with the statement: "Check him out. I think you'll like."

Well, she was wrong...I don't merely like his work...I LOVE it.

When I first opened her e-mail, I said about his artistic style: "Oh, wow, he's similar to that artist Paul and I first saw at Grove Park Gallery."

Then I whooped it up, excitedly, as I realized: He is THAT artist.

Leo Monahan is 84 years old and looks spectacular. I should know: I met him, personally, with friends, as we enjoyed coffee, at Well-Bred Café, in Weaverville. He came up to introduce himself, after having been told that I was the writer who posted a loving comment, regarding his work, on his new blog.

I invited him to join us. When asked, he told us of his rich past, as a Walt Disney employee, presumably using his gifts and talents in artistic endeavors, to the delight of children everywhere, I'm sure.

Now, he lives in Barnardsville, a neighboring town to Weaverville. His wife and he came out from Los Angeles, years ago; they found the home they'd delight in and moved in. But she still goes back and forth to Los Angeles (she's still got a foreign correspondent career).

But here's what I like about Leo Monahan's art. It's like nothing I've ever seen before. Yes, there are those who dabble in oil, water color, pastels, acrylics, but Leo is wildly unique: He cuts out his paper first, in the geometric shapes he needs... then layers... then paints his product.

His palette is rich and dramatic (except for his snowy white owl collection). A recent flurry of work emanated from the fact the cicadas (those bugs that live underground for twenty-seven years) were set to make explosive entry from their subterranean sojourn. (They make that buzzing noise on hot days.)

Oh, they weren't going to break the sound barrier in Western North Carolina (some say the mountain soil isn't conducive), and their emergence never made it as far north as New England, so we never heard their exiting rhapsody, either.

But Leo managed to capture them on canvas, in full array, in gorgeous, 3-D color...

The mountains of Asheville seem to inspire serious creativity, combined with whimsy: Leo Monahan's work comprises both.

Leo Monahan's work: Multi-dimensional and so original.
Here's his snowy white owl, against a backdrop of fall leaves.

Carl Sandburg's "Connemara"

Idyllic, almost-Asian artistry of form: an early Spring branch against a still pond, as fish lazily swim in eddies, lulled in the warming rays of the sun at Carl Sandburg's home in Connemara, Flat Rock, North Carolina.

As I grow older, I am comforted in the belief we're all connected, somehow. Walking the violet-studded grounds of Carl Sandburg's home, in spring, I see what he saw and witness the continuity of life: a bird flashing through dogwood branches; goats scampering on the hillsides (doubtless descendants of Sandburg's wife Lilian's prize herd); the bentwood chair atop the granite outcropping behind the house where the poet Sandburg spent hours writing. These are the woodlands he ambled. There, in that pastoral setting, he penned the memories of a lifetime.

When we visited this idyllic spot, I actually was motivated to try my own hand at poetry, for I envisioned Sandburg taking in the beauty of nature and penning his thoughts on that rock promontory he sought.

"Chain Reaction" (or "The Continuity of Life")

I want to know my deceased parents
Fulfill a lofty purpose at present.
After all, wherever they've gone,
I most likely will follow.
I don't envision either of them,
Sitting on some stupid cloud, playing a harp,
Or flitting from one celestial event to another
(Although my Mom would probably love that).

You see—if occupying that vapid state is all there is,
I don't want to be this ball of never-ending energy,
The one that never dies,
Just seeks a different host...
If that's the case, we're no different than cats
Who breed with their siblings, for God's sake!
(Oh, they're not to be blamed–
Incest requires one know the crime.)

I try hard to make sense of it all,
More so later in life, when the clock is ticking louder,
Reminding me that if I don't fathom the bigger reason
soon,
I join all the others on this conveyor belt of life,
Going Who-Knows-Where?, dressed only
With that catatonic look on their faces
That says: "I don't have a clue, either."
"I'm just along for the ride."

I suppose when my time comes,
My daughters will bury me, too.
At which point I'll join the cloud-hoppers.

But I refuse to carry a harp,
….And I definitely won't be singing.

Poetry's just another art form (along with writing and photography) to which I'm attracted in my later years. That'd odd because I never had much interest in it before. Maybe I'm maturing….. finally.

I encourage others to discover and nurture their own interests. The beauty? We don't have to be really good…We just need to try.

Connemara is the home to which Sandburg, "America's Poet," retreated at age 62. I found this ironic, in that I arrived in Asheville, at age 61. His home is now a National Historic Site to be appreciated by all.

Roadways Are Superb
(for the most part)

C oming from a home state that ranks fourth in the nation for "Poor Roads" (Rhode Island), we were continually struck by the efficiency of work crews and the beauty of North Carolina roads. And remember, North Carolina is a sizable state, whereas Rhode Island has a mere forty-eight miles from north to the south and thirty-seven miles from east to west.

Counties in other states have far greater distances to maintain than does our entire state.

But we are inordinately impressed with road construction and maintenance in North Carolina—all the more because so many of these steep and rutted mountain roads are barely accessible, in wintertime.

On North Carolina highways, we personally witnessed beautiful stone work adornment, fencing, and acres of purposely strewn wild flowers that delight the traveler for their aesthetic beauty, a nice touch in an era when most state highways are only ever concerned with utilitarian maintenance. Tree limbs are manicured so as not to encroach on the open space aside highways.

Prison workers are dispatched, as litter-pickers, daily, to keep highways clean. They appear in groups, marshaled by gun-toting officers, and we wonder why similar road clean-up can't be real-ized in our home state.

But it's the efficiency of road construction crews that most im-pressed us.

Case in point: Two years ago, in May, work crews arrived on Reems Creek Road, right outside our townhome complex. I cursed our luck that we were only going to be there for another month, during which time I figured we'd be dealing with the snarls and congestion that accompany similar Rhode Island road projects.

The road crew were there to resurface the road.

Now, here's the amazing part. In three days, workers complet-ed the job: a smooth black ribbon of a road, whose intersection with adjoining roads was another masterful accomplishment, for the connecting junctures appeared seamless.

This project in our home state would have taken months, a time during which everyone's patience would be tested.

I was so impressed, I asked the road crew supervisor how they finished so quickly and he answered: "We get a bonus for finishing ahead of time." I thought that idea brilliant.

In Rhode Island, I'm not aware of a penalty for road work not completed on time. In fact, jobs often go well beyond stated com-pletion dates, and then the job is done poorly, with the result the same old problems erupt, making us wonder if supervision ever occurs.

But I will say I found two minor aspects of North Carolina roadways disconcerting: The first is that damnable chirping sound assigned to some traffic lights in certain towns. In some cases, I commented: "After the first couple of chirps, I just wanted to shoot them."

Then, too, Asheville traffic lights seem much longer than those we experience elsewhere...longer even than those in Florida, the signature state that designs almost everything with older people's needs in mind. There, one expects overlong traffic lights for folks in walkers or with limited mobility to negotiate crosswalks.

But I'd frequently feel, in Asheville, and surrounding towns: "I'm aging a year, waiting for this traffic light to change."

Nonetheless, their road construction and maintenance are a pure joy and counter to what we Rhode Islanders experience in our home state. These confirm our suspicion: The North Carolina work ethic and product can be achieved elsewhere—most especially in a state as tiny as little Rhody.

Top Marketer Shows the Value of His "Other Craft"

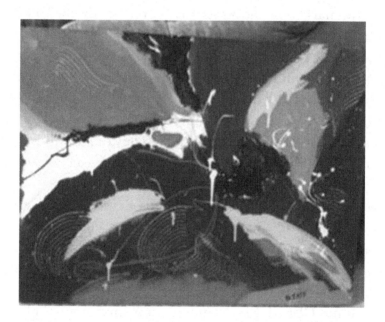

Asheville is a place where savvy marketers can showcase their work before an ever-growing population who appreciates their craft. Of course, many artists who settle there seem to almost despise the banal need to sell their wares. They'd prefer to isolate, reclusively, never needing to engage with the rest of the population, blessedly free to create their art pieces.

But necessity pushes them out, whether it be the Crafts Show for the region, held at the Asheville Civic Center, or in the various "Art Safaris" so popular in the region. In the latter, the artisans open their studios to the public who follow a map describing each artist and his or her location, allowing interested parties to view the artist at work.

But the artist who knows how to sell his wares? These folks are rare, indeed, in the market place. That's why I call attention to one as a bellwether for others who seek success.

After all, if the idea is to get one's art appreciated by the masses, why not market the daylights out of every medium? You'll never get known if you keep all the secrets about your great style (whether it's painting, writing, story-telling) to yourself and a select few.

As writer, I'm almost a whore when it comes to getting my stuff out there, to public notice.

At times, I've asked artist/painters in Asheville: "Do you have a business card or better yet–a website?" They demur and say, "Oh, no," (like I might have suggested they have a sexually transmitted disease –STD).

But folks who really know how to sell devise the best methods to draw attention to themselves and their products. And they go over—in a really big way.

Who's my Asheville nomination for Best Marketer? None other than that colorful painter whose artist studio is in the River Arts District, Jonas Gerard, for I've never seen anyone quite like him.

Case in point: When Paul and I went one spring day into downtown Asheville, Jonas Gerard held court, atop Pack Square (where the tall, granite obelisk is), under a white canopy, with a musician troupe he'd ostensibly hired to play accompanying music.

There, he spoke easily to the crowd while he painted a canvas right before them. He had the crowd rapt, and he reminded me of the Biblical Moses coming down from the Mount, to address the crowd.

But, instead of the tablet, Gerard mesmerized with his performance–a slap of the brush here... a dab there...a splash in the far corner (there are lots of these on his paintings), and after a half hour, or so, he was done, and offered the piece "for sale."

When some brave soul in the crowd asked, "If your paintings take literally minutes to produce, why do they command such a hefty price tag?" (of thousands).

Ever the quintessential, savvy marketer, Gerard replied: "Because buyers pay for my artistic skill developed over a lifetime."

I noted his brilliance. In one verbal sweep, he trounced the notion that any fool could mimic his talent.

I filed his answer away, to use in future salesmanship.

But as one who's been in sales all my life (teaching is sales with perhaps the arguably toughest audience—adolescents), I doff my cap, for I can only describe Gerard's ready response as "Pure Sales Nirvana." I thought: "This guy should market his marketing style, too (Sales 101), for the crowd bought his rationale (and he's right).

When an artist's work looks deceptively easy, it does so because he truly did develop his craft over many years. I know, for the same truth applies to writers. (See—I'm already copping Gerard's deft response.)

I can't tell you the number of people who believe that I sit at my computer, and the words flow, unbidden, from some font of creativity. They don't realize that I work at every piece, revising, honing, stripping away non-essentials, in hopes of achieving the best product.

This one chapter has gone through perhaps twenty re-writes.

My work, however, doesn't command thousands (a fact I hope to change).

In addition, Jonas Gerard's paintings are everywhere...at least in Asheville.

When Paul recovered from that terrible auto accident, at the rehabilitation center in Asheville, what did he see through blurry eyes, in the physical therapy room, each day? A Jonas Gerard painting, strategically placed, over the entryway.

Either Jonas Gerard made that painting a charitable contribution or it was possibly on loan.

More JG's were on the walls, at other locations throughout the facility.

That meant, as I wheeled Paul down corridors, we noted JG everywhere. It's safe to say: Paul recovered via Gerard's colorful palette.

His works of art could have created a subliminal connection, for when he got out, Paul asked: "Wanna buy a Jonas Gerard painting?"

When we dined in restaurants in town, who shared a repast with us? None other than the master, himself, whose works looked down on us from those walls, too.

JG's such a fabric of the community that friends sought to copy his style, in a painting (that's it, gracing the front of this chapter), without the talent, skill, pretense, or price of the master.

So, my advice to artists, anywhere: Step out from the shadows... It's a tough market out there. You need to devise methods to stand apart from the crowd. Not having a website or blogsite or fantastically interesting business cards just won't do, anymore.

Get your marketing game on. If you don't know how to do it, follow the lead of one who's made a mission out of it, in life—Jonas Gerard, my choice for savviest marketer in Asheville.

Maybe in the world.

Painting at top of this chapter was done by friends who tried to mimic Gerard's style. If you want to hire them, I'm sure they'll oblige. Contact me and I'll connect you.

You Can Wear Whatever You Want

A sheville attract lots of alternate-lifestyle-people (not talking personal relationships here)–people who just don't do the same things as others. That's one of the reasons we loved it there.

Here I am in a Big-Girl Tutu…

I was 8 years old when Mom put me in ballet school, with a female instructor who was super-glamorous. She was about 5'2," slim, wore tights, and had a little blonde bun atop her head (real ballerinas never have hair hanging in their faces).

I gotta say, my little kids' eyes continually fixated on her cross-stitched, black net stockings, encasing legs that were muscular but slim.

She was my idea of what I wanted to be–a glamorous ballerina. You know, the type that flits through the air in the perennial classic, "The Nutcracker." Or spins at the top of musical jewelry boxes, to a song like "Love Story."

Each week I'd go to my ballet lesson, then pirouette around the house, trying desperately to "toe," even tho' I hadn't the requisite footwear (you know, that squared-off ballet slipper, with the padded front). Or the experience and training.

None of that mattered to me: I considered myself one of those ethereal types, cavorting through the air, weightless, and lovely. (Even then, I was creating stories in my head.)

Then, my Mom got a look (a serious one) at the girl who was two years my senior, in those classes. Her legs were developing brutishly, with muscle-arrangements Mom never thought possible. Sinews looking strangely enough like the advance guard of varicose veins stretched in all directions, defying the graceful look of our instructor.

So Mom did what any caring Mom would do with a daughter poised on the edge of adolescence: She whipped me out of ballet...fast. ...saying "You're not going to have legs like Betsy's."

In a single move, my days on the stage were over. No more recitals...No more lovely tutus, encircling my waist...No more pretend toe shoes.

I was crushed.

So, when I met Dawn of Maid of Mars in the Verizon store, in Asheville, (she and I were similarly attending an instruction class for our 'Droid phones), I was thrilled, for she offered me an alternative: Yes, I could have a tutu, an adult one, no less, and because

I live in Asheville, no one would think my wearing a tutu, at age 67, "weird."

I didn't need toe shoes…I didn't need recitals…

In an instant, I could be brought back to my glorious days in that dance studio, via my very own adult-size-tutu (she makes tutus on demand, for the little crowd, too). Dawn even makes headgear (one looks like variegated plumage.), aprons, etc…anything one can dream up with fabric and all sorts of accessories (leather, feathers, etc.).

So, I continually sing Dawn's praises, for she offers a service for a public I'm sure is out there.

After all, I'm a closet ballerina…been one for years.

And remember—In Asheville, there are few bounds restricting folks, so everyone (male, female, transgender, young, old, in-between) can wear them. I might wear mine to meet a friend for lunch, at Earthfare, in Asheville.

Or I might wear mine, just going about, on errands, in Warwick, Rhode Island, and measure the different reaction.

Here's Maid of Mars's Etsy shop to order a specially-made gift for a little (or big) girl or boy…Remember, we're all free-er now: http://www.etsy.com/shop/thuviamaidofmars

Silver Is "the New Black"

Remember the Peanuts cartoon character with the naturally-curly, red hair– Frieda? Well...that's me...It's just I didn't know I had naturally curly hair 'til recently.

When the lights go up following a movie, on any afternoon, in cinemas across Asheville, one notes a sea of white...silver...pewter, atop heads of many movie-goers. That landscape makes me ever so comfortable...

But my comfort didn't come easily....

I wrestled with it for years...whether or not to continue bleaching my hair the blonde color I opted for, at the tender age of 28. There was my mother's statement when I was 48: "Colleen, why don't you stop coloring your hair and let it go back to the shade it was?" I wondered: Was she being mean or did she really think my hair could revert to the rich mahogany/chestnut mix it was when I was a young woman?

The reality is: I've spent whole decades of my life punishing my hair... brutalizing it, in fact. If I'd heard this type of chemical pollution happened anywhere else—besides my head—I'd be the first in line with a sign, protesting.

For years, I sat through the process whereby my hairstylist pulled my hair strands through a rubber perforated cap (a sieve-like bonnet), and then painted those same strands with bleach.

The fact that she wore rubber gloves to protect her own skin should have concerned me, but the only time it did was when I was pregnant. Even then, I pooh-poohed my concern, saying: "Well, they wouldn't allow these products for pregnant women, if they weren't safe."

My naivete makes me shudder.

This hair coloring process was called "frosting," as if giving it a confectionary name would make it more palatable—or less toxic. That technique was all the rage.

One time the cap slipped and the process left me with alternating light/dark bands, the signature look of a skunk, with the entire front row framing the face untouched and dark, against the bleached section. I had to sit through a re-do.

And I did, for I was like a drug addict. I couldn't stop. My addiction went on for the next forty years.

When I first came to Asheville, I tried desperately to find a hair stylist who'd do me the supreme favor of managing my macabre ritual with the hair products I'd used in my home state. I even provided stylists with the same color code number and name of the products she used.

Asheville response? "We don't do that here."

I remember thinking, "Damn purists."

Oh, they offered supposed natural product alternatives but nothing akin to the alleged poison I'd been using. I feared I'd have to "go underground" to get what some in Asheville consider "illegal drugs."

Then a strange thing happened: I began to wonder what would happen if I ceased the assault altogether. Perhaps I could ease into aging, after all. Maybe I wouldn't have dull, gun-metal grey hair. Maybe I'd have the polished pewter locks my Nana did, a lady that

I, as a young child, set up in a back yard chair, unpinning her bun, allowing her waist-length hair to tumble.

On those occasions, I began the hundred stroke ritual she promised would make anyone's hair shine. When I finished, she'd take a quarter out of her apron pocket and hand it to me, saying in her Cockney accent (dropping the h's): "Ere's a quarter, Colleen..." I'd thank her, and when she didn't notice, deposit it right back in her pocket for our next session.

"Yep," I noted, "She had beautiful hair" (but then again, she was my Nana).

With her in mind, I made my decision: I'd honor her memory and join folks in this town who accept their aging gracefully. With that, I went cold turkey and stopped.... no more bleaching...no more foils.

Now, here's the kicker: My natural hair gets rave reviews. That, alone, is pretty funny, since no one praised the frosted version, in years...

An added bonus? My hair's naturally curly. Once I ceased stripping the strands... stopped exposing them to chemicals... they began dancing around my head, in ringlets and curves... happy as can be.

I find this all truly amazing.

The picture below is a contemporary of mine who knew the beauty of "natural" way before I did: Diana Stone is a Leicester psychologist and Open Heart Meditation instructor whom I'd met at Staples (I stopped her mid-store to praise her hair).

Yep...Diana and I–two women in Asheville who accept our aging gracefully.

My question? "Why didn't I know, years ago, how much easier life could be?"

Above is Diana Stone, a smart lady who knows the value of a monochromatic black outfit to set off her glorious locks.

Two Can Eat Out as Cheaply as One (in New England)

The above Billagio's dish is so smothered in cheese, even I don't know what I ordered...

I know I shouldn't do this (and you'll find out what 'this' is,) for I had a wise neighbor back in Rhode Island, much older than I, who taught me a valuable lesson in life: *If you find something good, don't share it with another.*

Know what? He was right, but at the time, I was furious with him.

You see, I'd asked him for the name of the young boy who did odd jobs for him, and he hemmed and hawed..."Couldn't recall"...Or he told me he'd "call me later, when it came to him." But he never did...

I figured the reason out, via another neighbor incident.

I hired a young girl in the neighborhood to clean my house and babysit. Then, I stupidly raved about her to a woman who lived across the street from me. What happened? That woman poached my girl and began calling her for her needs (ahead of me).

Upshot? I lost the girl as my helper.

You know the TV show "2 Broke Girls"? Well, I don't really know it, aside from my viewing it once, during its first season. Apparently, the story line revolves around two young women (with wickedly disparate passions) who come together out of necessity.

In short, they're without funds, so they move in, together, for mutual survival.

Well, in a way, my husband and I cop their frugality, when eating out...except we're not young girls and we're not really "broke." We just like to see how much of a bang for our buck we can get for our money.

As two, money-conscious seniors, we make a real mission of finding the best bargains in eating out in Asheville. We do this is Rhode Island, too.

Here's our hands-down (for now) best restaurant in Asheville for sharing a decent-sized, good meal... cheaply.

Bellagio's in Woodfin.

Yep...It's "Italian" and considering we're from Rhode Island, former home of alleged infamous Mafia, we know and can assess good Italian food.

Here's the beauty of this place: We order one full-breasted, chicken parmigiana, smothered in mozzarella cheese; it comes to us, piping hot, atop a huge plateful of spaghetti. Alongside it are a Greek salad (don't know why it's Greek in an Italian restaurant but it's yummy), and garlic bread (yep, we split that, too).

Cost to us, for dinner? $16.00 for sit-down, full dinner, tax and tip.

In contrast, a mere shared sandwich at Greenlife Grocery Store (owned by Whole Foods), two cups of soup (at special price since each comes with half sandwich,) costs us $15.00.

For that, we stand as we await our order, then go through a check-out line, and carry our food up to the dining room where we wrestle others for a table.

Sometimes, there's a wait.

So, all in all, we find the best bang for our senior buck is Bellagio's.

But "Shhhhhhh..." Don't tell anyone else, for I know what will happen. Bellagio's will be mobbed (and not by the Mafia); we won't be able to get a table; and their prices will go up.

A lesson I learned long ago from my neighbor that I'm obviously ignoring.

What's our favorite inexpensive meal spot in Rhode Island for a quick bite and fun with owner Ross, and counter women Ashley and Savannah? Tio Mateo, in East Greenwich, where we get two big bowls of excellent soup, with chips, a side of fresh fruit, and a soft drink for $13.00.

It's a Dog's World ...Unless You've Got a Cat

Remember that Priceline commercial on TV where "Big Bang Theory's Kaley Cuoco appears, as newscaster, interviewing a young man wearing a cat t-shirt, at Feline Convention? She asks the convention-goer: "So where's your furry friend?" to which he answers, "I don't have one."

At that, Kaley dead-pans to her TV crew, registering silent disbelief. She can't understand a man whose shirt professes to be "All about cats," doesn't have one.

I know how it feels to be one of a pet-less minority, for the fact Paul and I lived in a town (Asheville) where it seems everyone MUST have a dog, for 85% of this town's population is "All about Dogs."

Another 15% goes the feline route. (I have no idea if my figures are correct!)

If you're "sans pet," here, it's like being a heterosexual, single woman, in an all-male, gay town...You're in a distinct minority.

I was the only pet-less one, at a party I attended my first year, in Asheville.

Upon our arrival, I was invited to a women's party. Oh, it was magnificent—a post- Thanksgiving get-together for those of us who missed family on that auspicious occasion... in whatever states we were from.

Everyone at that party had a dog (or two)...except me.

When folks arrived at the hostess's home, they opened car doors to release unfettered pets who proceeded to bound across her lawn. They all seemed to know one another, too (the pets, that is), greeting each other with big, slobbering kisses.

I looked about: Shitzhugh's, labs, beagles, and border collies were everywhere.

When eyes met eyes, it was "Mano – A-ni-mo"...And the wild exclamations, such as "Oh, he's so cute"..."Look at those eyes!" Then again, "Is it a girl? "Oh...I see...It's a male" (all laugh).

Then the purring...the petting...the "Awwwing" over everyone's version of doggie wonder.

I never saw anything like it...Not even when we were all mothers at a much earlier point in life, cooing over each other's infants.

Quite simply–We never gave each other's babies such rapt adoration.

It got me to thinking. Of course we didn't. It's so much easier loving furry friends.

We're older now...We know the score...We've learned in life.

Babies are one-sided. Older "kids" are even worse. They're not as cute and they're still taking...or trying to take.

In life, we gave...gave...and gave. They all took...continually.

We waited years 'til the tables turned. In some cases, that never happened.

No... dogs and cats are waaaayyy more reciprocal. And considering the IQ of this town of Asheville (I'll warrant it's a notch above the average!), people here came to that conclusion, waaaayyyy earlier.

So, free advice? If you're settling in Asheville, get a dog or two. I mean, look around and see how pets rule. Don't believe me? Note the high-end pet surgical hospital with state-of-the-art, glass-fronted operating rooms looking out onto Merrimon Ave., in Woodfin. I'll warrant that beats out surgical centers for humans in other towns.

Some pet clinics offer pet therapy, too, and dental services, at a time when some seniors eschew such dental treatment for themselves, as luxury. A friend on a recent outing shared with me that she had to get back home and minister to her pet, because her dog "had nine teeth pulled that day," at the clinic.

I'll admit to tamping down the image of her pooch being fitted for a partial; I didn't want to appear insensitive, since I value her as good friend, but I wonder about friends who bypass their own dental needs, while shelling out for pets.

Pet owners exhibit serious commitment to pets in this town and a magazine like *Critter* dispenses free advice to all who are pet-challenged.

So, I repeat: In Asheville, you better have a pet...or two.

Here's the pet clinic in Woodfin whose shiny, steel, state-of-the-art equipment is just behind the wall of glass. There are pet ambulances, too, whenever a furry one suffers deep distress. What a town!

True Grits and Southern Gentility

If you're in the South for any length of time, you're bound to learn of certain people's blind adherence to a food similar in appearance and color to cream-of-rice cereal (without the lumps). Oftentimes butter and cheese is added to its base (which guarantees anything be good, in my book), and I've seen this dish teamed with peppers, zucchini, and onions.

Its less-than-desirable name is "grits" and the flat-out favorite food pairing for this creamy porridge (among Southerners) is shrimp.

To many Southerners, shrimp and grits is gustatory nirvana.

I recall my first tasting of this concoction which prompted my query: "Why are Southern folk so crazy for this stuff?" To me, even with the additives, it was bland. A crunchy shrimp or two couldn't convert me to a believer. But since that time, I've come to accept that loving that dish is really a Southern thing; it doesn't need any more explanation than that. I don't always understand why it works, but it does…pure and simple.

In this laid-back, beautiful western North Carolina region, where nature and greeners come together, "Life is good," as the t-shirts say.

People smile often; men still hold doors for women; and "Allow me, ma'am" is a frequent request to serve. In short, western North Carolina offers a much slower pace, one defined by graciousness and respect, and it's a key reason we settled there.

And in the oddest instance of all, people look each other in the eye, as they acknowledge one other, saying "Hello, Ma'am" or "Hello Sir." They never effect that peculiar northern posture of avoiding eye contact, 'lest one invite unwarranted interaction.

When folks engage, they're inordinately accommodating to one another, too, because simple graciousness (long disappeared in the Northeast) is a way of life. Patience is not just a virtue here; it's prescribed ritual.

But sometimes that famous Southern gentility can bring a Northerner to madness.

I remember the time I was in line (of six deep) at a Dollar General Store, in late December, and the woman being waited on asked the lone store clerk if the store carried Christmas ribbon.

The clerk told her, "Yes, ma'am—in row 6." The clerk then followed up with: "Would you like me to wait while you go down and get what you need?"

Now, I stood incredulous, at the thought of the long train of customers, cooling our heels, as this lone shopper visited the aisle she'd missed, to rummage through bins for ribbon. I had to shut myself up, cautioning: "Now, come on...this is a reason you like it here. It's never the fevered pitch of life in the Northeast, and that comes with a price—even if the price is insane, by northern standards."

I recall, too, the time Paul and I brought my younger daughter to William & Mary, in Williamsburg, Virginia, for her junior year of college. We'd just made a seven hundred mile trip in Paul's Ford truck jammed with all her essential belongings. She sat on the hard portion of the seat between him and me, while I tried to accommodate my 5'9" frame to the remaining space, my position made more uncomfortable in that my foot was encased in a cast, the result of a recent surgery.

At the school, we arrived late, which meant she missed orientation and guide direction.

The next morning we moved her into her assigned room and then toured the beautiful town of Williamsburg, a colonial bastion steeped in history and charm. Following that, my daughter met up with friends, and we proceeded to leave. We had a long drive home.

Paul left me, curbside, while he went for the truck. As Paul pulled up, a young man stepped briskly towards me. Fearing his intentions, I readied my crutch in self-defense mode, poised to batter him, similar to Ruth Buzzi 's bun-haired, older woman on the late 1960's "Rowan and Martin's Laugh-In" television show, who beat off the old man's advances with her purse.

But just as we stood almost face-to-face, he shot ahead, grabbed the door handle of the truck, opened it wide and invited me to step up, saying "Ma'am...?" (in the sweetest Sir Walter Raleigh kind of way), while I sheepishly thanked him. He was simply the not-so-rare breed of young man (in the South) who steps up to help a woman in distress.

So...grits...gentility...charm...It's a Southern thing... And we women love it (Well, not the grits part, maybe....).

In Asheville, Police Respond (Too) Quickly

He looks innocent enough...doesn't he? Don't believe it. He'll call the cops on me, in a heartbeat.

There's a spot right outside Greenlife grocery store, on Merrimon Ave., in Asheville, that's marked forever, with a sign warning about overlong parking, due to me (perhaps?). It happened a few years back, on the night of the Hollywood Oscars, when a group of us got together for a party.

My best North Carolina friend, Cynthia, and I decided to meet at Greenlife's and then go to a fringe region of Asheville where another friend was hosting an Oscar Party.

We picked up goodies for the party, stashed my car in the lot, and left. We'd come back later, to retrieve my car. The plan seemed a good one.

Well, for the next several hours, we whooped it up, hysterically laughing, voting Siskel and Ebert style for "Best Actor"..." Best Movie"..."Best Whatever." We even cast votes on paper ballots the hostess provided.

Apparently, during the course of the evening, my cell phone rang twice, but I never heard it…Too much going on. We tend to be a frenzied group.

Anyway, we said our "Goodnights" and proceeded to the grocery store. Cynthia dropped me off, and I then took my own car, for the last leg of the journey. Since I was fifteen minutes away from home, I decided to call Paul, suspecting he was probably asleep on the couch.

But that was So-Not-the-Case.

The voice that met me on the other end sounded frantic. "Where are you?" he said.

"What do you mean, where am I? I'm in my car heading home," I replied.

Then, he added: "Well, I've got the police here and I've just filed a Missing Person Report."

I thought he was kidding, until he put an officer on. "Ma'am," said she…"Are you all right?"

I answered, "Yes, of course…What's the problem?"

Her reply: "Well, when your husband tried to reach you twice, he got worried, and called us. He apparently feared you'd gone off-road, ending up in a ditch. We're in your kitchen right now."

Mortified, I told them I'd be right there.

I then called my friend who was in her car, somewhere behind me. When I told her what happened, Cynthia said, "Oh, yes, I saw two police cars tailing you (OJ-Bronco-Chase -style), as you left the parking lot. I wondered what was up."

It wasn't bad enough that my husband called Weaverville Police (we live in Weaverville), but apparently that department contacted Buncombe County Police. Now, the whole regional force was looking for me!!!

I know that because I next got a call from the Buncombe County dispatch officer who asked: "Ma'am, are you all right?"

I want to say "No...I'm not all right. In a panic, my crazy partner directed police everywhere to find me... all because I somehow missed the magical curfew he created in his head."

More insane than that: They all did it.

The real irony: In any other town/city across America, a person must be missing *two whole days* before officials do anything. But not in Asheville.

Be forewarned: If you live in Asheville, or surrounding regions, check in with your mate, if you're out later than expected, for they get into real trouble if they're left alone too long.

Yoga and Yogis Are Everywhere

It's my fault: I'd threatened it for years: I told everyone I was going to enroll in Yoga classes.

I've always regarded Yoga Folk as having a certain inner peace I want. They're the ones I see along green places, in nature, communing, as they contort their bodies in pretzel-like fashion. They never care about anyone watching...

The need to perform physically fluid movement should have been a giveaway, as to why Yoga might not work for me.

To think I could fashion my body in modes that only work for children, Cirque de Soleil gymnasts, or those who've been following the lifestyle for years was my undoing.

In the Christmas of the final year Paul and I lived in Asheville, my younger daughter gave me a thirty day pass to a Yoga spa in Asheville. And because she wanted me to be prepared for the occasion, she gave me the padded floor mat to go along with that pass.

All I needed to do was show up. With that, I went to my first-ever class.

Upon entry to the building, I was directed to put my things (jacket, purse) in a cubby, along the wall. Having done that, I proceeded to the big room where some thirty people were already convened, their mats strategically spread out... water bottles nearby.

As I walked across the floor, a woman closest to the door (self-appointed monitor, perhaps?) shouted, "Woah...Your shoes!" I thought she meant I had toilet paper stuck to one (I'd gone to the ladies' room) and glanced down.

Seeing nothing wrong, I said "Please?"

She answered: "No shoes in this room." Just that. A short... swift, non-welcome to one who'd broken a cardinal rule of Yoga...I wondered: "I thought these were gentle folk...What gives with the attitude?"

From that point on, it was "Pure awful."

The instructor seemed nice enough. Told how much he admired the person for whom he Yoga-substituted that day...how we students had to build a stable base before we climbed to the heights of Yoga we'd achieve. His voice was soothingly hypnotic.

I took my place in the last row. When we did warm-up moves, our guru directed us to finger the wall (to unlock our shoulders), and since I was at the only unoccupied area in a crowded room, I had little wall space.

I'd only learn my "stuck status" when he called out the directive to turn and repeat the movement in the other direction.

I couldn't...my bit of wall space ended and a glass door presented.

In Lucille Ball fashion, I stood clueless, hoping no one noticed.

Actually, no one did, for my neighbors were all in some kind of Zen state.

Then we got into positions. On command, all around me, men and women dropped down on the mats and stretched out, holding positions akin to push-up's without movement. They held themselves up, defying gravity, with their hands and feet planted firmly on the floor. I marveled at their athleticism.

But I wondered: "Why the Hell did the girl at the desk suggest this class to me?"

I knew, too: "If this is Beginners' Yoga, I'm no candidate!"

For most of thirty minutes, I just stood. I'd given up all pretense of trying to follow his directive, as he called out, "Maintain your downward facing dog position."

Whenever they hit the mats (often), I became the one vertical in the room, besides him.

At one point, he quietly sidled up to me and asked: "Are you all right?" (probably trying to find out if I were having one of those silent heart attacks we hear about).

I said, "Oh, yes, I'm just a beginner."

What I wanted to say was: "No...I'm not OK...I've got MS, and I can't even begin to do these poses. In fact, I question whether any body *should*."

Instead, after another few minutes, I simply rolled up my mat and tip-toed out...stopping by the desk to ask: "Is this really Beginners' Yoga?"

The girl at the desk appeared stunned. She apologized for whoever suggested this class might work for me. She's now telling me about "Gentle Yoga," (as opposed to "Tough Yoga").

While this was my maiden entry into the world of Yoga, I found my comfort zone, ultimately, and continued in Asheville, and then, back in Rhode Island, enjoying it immensely. I got any number of friends involved who became Yoga folks, too.

But, it is that Asheville Yoga class that is responsible for a great swath of us (in Rhode Island) becoming far more fluid in our movement.

Ironically, some have become almost yogis and are giving commands in their own right.

I also found that Yogis offer reduced rates—some as low as $3.00 a class– in all locations (church halls and senior residences), both in Rhode Island and Asheville. Then, too, fitness clubs, like LA Fitness where Paul and I paid $40.00 a month for couples' membership allows access to all equipment, pool, spinning and Yoga classes, etc.

The only difference between Yoga people in Asheville and Rhode Island? Asheville's are holding positions in supermarkets, bank lines, etc. Uninhibited; they optimize every moment of living.

To me, this becomes "Intense Yoga."

Photo at top of this chapter is the beautiful studio in Asheville where I began, a studio who can now claim many Rhode Islanders as avowed followers in that I introduced friends back home to Yoga. They continue today.

Continuing Yoga...The Fart Heard 'Round the (Yoga) World

I just finished my fourth Yoga class (but it's really my third, since I unceremoniously bolted, from my first class).

I crawled to the get-ready-to-leave bench, still part of this Yoga School's 30 day/$60.00 special, whereby the business hopes to hook me as part of its new generation of Yoga diehards.

But I'm exhausted. I simply can't believe this thing is so-o hard (for me).

Our instructor for this class is different (they all are.) He started out, telling us the class was "For Beginners" but not to be fooled. "Beginner Yoga doesn't mean it's easy."

Since I want "Easy Yoga," I make a mental note to look that up, in the school's on-line schedule.

Next, he goes into the meaning of "Dialogue," saying "conversation happens when one's body parts talk to each other."

Unlike my other teachers, he didn't play any soothing music, for us, either...Probably wanted to facilitate us in hearing our bodies "talk."

Well, on that score, I'll say this: By the end of class, my body parts were definitely talking...They were swearing and hollering, too, even using the F bomb, as in "What the F are we doing here with a bunch that was obviously raised on this pablum?"

Some were talking in tongues, too, and they weren't taking turns, either.

So, I dialogued back with my body and tried to give it some insight. Here's what I said:

"I think I finally know why Yoga's so hard for us (remember—I'm talking to my body): First off, we've got MS, so we're not on a level playing field with others; our muscles scream when extended and they're decidedly weaker than others.'

"Next, we're dyslexic, so every time we nail a position (and we're proud), Yoga Prof. takes away our glory and calls out, meanly, to reverse the position. We get all mixed up.

"Then, too, we react slowly to drill-sergeant commands. (Yoga instructors always call out commands.) We especially liked it (sarcastic) when today's guru had us hold a tough pose, and then forgot about us, while he gave a 14-year-old boy (even more newbie than I) his personal attention and encouragement." That's when we (body and I) dropped down on our mat, when the quivering in our legs took on spastic proportions.

"Finally, at 67, we're older, so movements, once fluid, are 'staccato' at best, 'impossible,' at worst."

What did we enjoy? When someone farted. It had to happen... with all this stretching and exposing bodies to openness.

We knew not to dissolve into hysteria, for we needed to conserve energy, if for no other reason than to stagger out, at the end of class, in some kind of upright position.

But the veiled fart was the first real funny thing that's happened in Yoga Town.

Following class, I met my first Yoga friend—Lisa– who told me that this is her third year in Beginner Yoga. I was stunned. That's when I realized: Yoga's not like other schools.

We know, too: There's no shame being in Beginner Yoga... maybe forever.

Even so, I'm looking up Easy Yoga.

Now, if I can just hobble on out to my car……

P.S. I wrote this chapter two years ago and only learned this year that another woman recently wrote a similar article about a yoga fart that went viral (the article did—not the fart). Yep, everybody thought her piece hysterical. I believe she posted it in Reddit.

As author, I was beaten to the altar by one of the tech-savvy, younger crowd.

Will I ever learn the necessity of mastering social media?

You Can Celebrate Friends
"Downton Abbey" Style

I saw a card in a shop in Black Mountain, a town some miles out from Asheville, that said: "Value your girlfriends"…Inside, it says "Because that's who'll be with you, at the end."

So true….After all, we all know how "life"—or more specifically "death" works. (Spoiler Alert: men shouldn't read beyond here.)

It's a scientific fact: Women outlive men, often by more than a decade. I know the "*sans partner*" situation well. As stated, by 43, I'd divorced one husband and buried two more.

When I wasn't sobbing (or recovering), I referred to myself as "The Black Widow... without the Money." And because I know single-hood, I value friends and make sure I spend quality time with them.

I had a chance to do that, recently, for a friend's birthday. Admittedly, it wasn't tough duty. Her husband rented a posh, over-sized end room, with sweeping views, at the Biltmore Inn, for an occasion that's become his wife's annual "Night to howl" with female friends.

Now, I've personally never been to the Biltmore Inn, before, because "Why would I?" I owned a perfectly lovely condo in Weaverville and I got my Biltmore fix a-plenty. But I have to say: With my recent winter visit, I was wildly impressed.

Sure I'd been to the duck pond...the barn...the House...I've biked the pathways. But I'd never been to the Inn.

On this occasion, a friend and I drove along tracks of open land, in the late afternoon, as the sun bathed all in a warm glow, and deer cavorted across the hills. The few cars ahead of us, on the roadway, ground to a stop, mesmerized by the animals' antics, while I quipped "those deer are probably mechanized."

Then we sucked in our breath. The Inn stood high and majestic, atop a prominent hill.

We parked and entered via a door opened by an older gentleman (in full livery?). Now, maybe it's the Downton Abbey Effect, or gracious Bert in his role as official greeter, but I swear: As we stepped over that threshold, we entered a world of gentility.

In our friend's room, we enjoyed drinks and snacks (trays and wine goblets were provided by the Inn) and raved about the view. Then we headed down to the library/lounge for an informal meal.

Now, here's the thing about us women: We're careful spenders (but good tippers). A friend and I shared a burger (they're huge); it came with fries; she had coffee and I had water. Our bill? Mine-$9.75; hers– $11+ (without tip)...Seriously...

All this grandeur...the beauty of the wild backdrop...the mountains rising in the distance...the paneled library replete with books no one probably reads....the gorgeous room with sweeping ceiling-to-floor drapes...the food...with tip—for one low price!!!

Her husband's bill (remember, the room's his birthday treat for her)? $109.00. He paid the vastly-reduced rate in late January, for pass-holders who meet other qualifications such as type of room, occupancy rate, day of week, pass-holder status. If you can't get bargain rates this winter, consider reserving ahead for next year.

After dinner and a proper howling at the full moon, outdoors, the rest of us got in our cars and wended our way across the moonlit roadways of the estate, while the Birthday Girl went upstairs to sink into the deep pile of her beautiful bed.

So, my takeaway: Share the love: Not just on Valentine's Day. If your partner/spouse's birthday falls in one of these tourist off-months, consider it a boon...Rent a room/night at Biltmore Inn for a Friends' Party, when prices are drastically-reduced.

That's reason enough, right there, to howl.

P.S. Now that I think of this, it might be a grand idea to duplicate this practice in Rhode Island, with girlfriends renting a room at one of our Newport hotels, with its own glorious view...spectacular food, etc. We'll just have to get our own "Bert, the doorman."

Picture of gentility—Bert– Biltmore Inn's gracious doorman when I was there. So "Downton Abbey"...

Three S's and WSJ...
for $50.00 a Month

I'm a bargain hunter. That means: I comparison-shop. For instance, when I needed to align with an indoor place for regular work-out's (and I don't mean the usual gym scene), I looked for indoor swimming pools, in Asheville.

Everyone told me to go to the downtown YMCA. But because I find Y's frequently too busy for my personal taste, I looked for alternatives.

I found what I needed at Renaissance Hotel, in downtown Asheville, which provided pure swimmer's nirvana.

In Rhode Island, I buy a pass for the University of Rhode Island's indoor pool.

First off, the Renaissance pool is one enormous body of salt water where I often swam alone. Pure, unbridled swimming...a bubbling hot tub, nearby, a small and unobtrusive women's changing area, with lockers and showers (two, to be exact).

Since the swimming pool is primarily for hotel guests, the facility even provides towels. If you go when the supply on shelves is just replenished, you might even get still-warm towels. What a treat!

The expanse of clear blue, saline water stretches endlessly. I don goggles and descend the steps. I never need suffer the damnable "share the lane" policy often required in health clubs that have pools, a situation I fear for the possibility I'll be struck with an errant swimmer's elbow.

In fact, often, I'm the only swimmer in the pool. (That might change with this book's coming out.)

When I complete my swim routine (thirty minutes), I dip into the hot tub to loosen my muscles. Following that, I take a chair at one of the many beside-the-pool tables and proceed to read the Wall St. Journal, while munching on an apple. Both the newspaper and fruit are courtesy of the hotel and are provided in the gym area, behind a glass wall.

So, swim...snack...and shower, plus Wall St. Journal...all included in the price.

After the work-out and clean-up, Paul and I head out for lunch. And because we're frequent food shoppers (since we prefer fresh food and we have the time to shop daily), we combine eating lunch with grocery-shopping.

Food shopping is the one area in Asheville and Rhode Island I find lacking, but it's not for the reasons grocery store managers would think. (They and the chains that hire them should be reading this book that speaks to what seniors want in their food shopping.)

The salt water pool at Renaissance Hotel in downtown Asheville...yards and yards of silky, uninterrupted water with a lovely bank of windows on two sides, so one never feels closed in.

Food Shopping Fun...
But Could Be Better

In Rhode Island, we go to Whole Foods for the organic food we choose.

But choices of organic food vendors widens, when we're in Asheville, North Carolina.

For lunch, we used to go to Greenlife (it's a closet Whole Foods that kept its name, but I guess now it's morphed again into Amazon), but once it got taken over by Whole Foods, we noted real changes. No more special discounts for Seniors...Never one for Military... Sandwiches appeared smaller and our bill seemed to go up.

Maybe Amazon will change all this.

Paul and I used to split a sandwich (their hot paninis were huge) which we paired with a cup of soup for each. If we got cups of water from the giant glass urn in the dining area, we kept our bill down.

But just like a fickle public everywhere, we changed loyalties and went with another.

Earth Fare got us next. We discovered we could eat better and cheaper, with each of us getting half a sandwich and cup of soup, then using our Military discount of 15% (they offer Senior discount, too, but you can't combine) to pare down our bill. We could further reap rewards if we used our Tomato Bank money, whereby we've bought special items at the store that give us points toward cash value.

Now, Earth Fare has changed those everyday discounts, designating Mondays as Senior Discount Day, with Military Discount on Thursdays. How is that a problem for seniors? We usually forget which days are what and find ourselves missing out on the savings. Their Healthy Rewards program (the old Tomato Bank program), however, operates every day.

Basically, we enjoyed the atmosphere of Earth Fare, too, with ample seating space for eating, and we wondered why more stores don't provide this. The newer food markets on Merrimon Avenue apparently never asked customers "What do you want from your grocery store?" for strangely absent from these state-of-the-art emporiums are attractive, spacious eating areas.

If asked, most seniors I know would have said: "Good prices and an attractive eating area."

Why? Paul and I choose our shopping venue based on that combination. We simply don't understand a huge food store providing minimal space for customers to eat, almost hiding them behind a dividing wall that paradoxically suggests, in its mural, the vastness of the Blue Ridge Mountains.

Or stores that provide unappealing, front-of-store dining areas in the visual field of shoppers standing in check-out lines, a situation we find in Rhode Island, as well.

We want to know why in-store eating is discouraged and wonder, too, why food stores can't offer aesthetically-appealing areas, clean and well-maintained (because some aren't and we stopped going to some for that very reason).

We can't understand managerial staff not assigning staff to clean tables after each diner leaves.

We like dining areas well-lighted with windows or even skylights providing natural light. Maybe live plants and real flowers in planters (akin to a garden) for aesthetic effect.

There are other preferences we have, too. I used to love it when Earth Fare alerted me to special deals. They pinged me on my cell phone (I gave them my e-mail and phone number,) and I gotta say: I liked their instant messages better than those from family. Why? Unlike family, Earth Fare was giving me something, with their notice, such as a bake-at-home pizza for half price or a real deal on chocolates, at Easter time.

Similarity to Whole Foods? Earth Fare provides bite-sized, food sample stations throughout the store, allowing shoppers to graze as we shop.

And of course, the food is all-natural.

We especially liked Earth Fare's hot bar or cold salad bar for its variety and quality.

But aesthetic charms are not what gets us in the door. As with "All Things Business," it's the practical savings Earth Fare offers. If all things are equal in the natural food emporiums (and they allegedly are), we're swayed by Senior and Military discounts and that Tomato Bank (now Healthy Rewards) program.

But, remember: We, the public (especially seniors), are fickle. If we note another competitor on the horizon who begins to offer more, we'll ditch our supposed favorites in a heartbeat.

In the meantime, Earth Fare: Establish a beachhead in Rhode Island and open a store, here. And go back to pinging me. I loved your instant messages.

Short of that: I want Whole Foods (now Amazon) to give the same shopper deals (Senior and Military discounts, Ping-me-deals, Tomato Bank).

In other words, I want Whole Foods to love their customers... the way Earth Fare used to (discounts honored *every* day.)

Heart-Stopping Medical Folk

I'd rounded the bend and was coming up the hill, doing a fast-clip walk and noted several people all clumped together on the footpath, ahead, and I recall thinking: "Well, that's a terrible place to socialize...Don't they see me coming? I'll have to walk right through them or around. How rude of them to hog the path!"

I never noted the guy on the ground.

When I was almost upon them, at the crest of the hill, a woman said, "We tried to call you..." I was confused and still not understanding, and then I looked down. The guy on the ground was Paul, sitting there, bloodied and shaken. Someone had already called Rescue.

I recall thinking: "OK, this has to stop. I don't know how many more of these occasions I can take..." It had been three years (almost to the day), since Paul went in an ambulance to a local hospital, with that broken neck.

Today's injuries looked far worse than they were. Apparently, he'd tripped on a rock in the path and then went flying. His head, hands and knees were all ripped up.

But I just stood, dazed. I guess the word "Rescue" brought it all back.

When again, the woman said, "You don't have your cell phone with you?" I nodded "No, I don't." It's odd, too, that I didn't, for I usually carry it with me. She then said "Well, when you get it, you'll note a couple of calls from us."

I still stood, confused as to what happened.

When we had nothing to sop up the blood from his cuts, one lady in a "C'est La Vie" t-shirt offered what she carried in her car for child emergencies—a roll of toilet paper. She apologized for nothing more medic-worthy, while Paul joked (thankfully, he never loses his sense of humor) that he wasn't fussy...He'd use it.

I filed away her practice, thinking: "Good idea" (to travel with a roll in the car).

When the Emergency Medical Squad (EMS) arrived, they all hovered over him and assessed his condition, while I was struck by something else: They were all GQ-Worthy Men who could have each graced a Hunk Calendar (you know—Mr. May....Mr. March ..those magazines where they show off their pecs).

It was as if these men, wearing those crazy, mustard-colored overalls with suspenders, all stepped off a movie set.

I began to wonder: In Asheville, is there a minimum bar of gorgeous for one to be on the EMS Team? I didn't share my thoughts, for they seemed wildly-inappropriate, considering the scenario (but really, now, I knew Paul wasn't seriously-injured).

But, possibly, others would think me shallow.

Furthermore, let's face it: We older women aren't even supposed to think like that.

But I repeat: These guys were over-the-top-handsome, so much so that if I were young, and in the market for a mate, I might self-inflict, just for the chance to have them attend me.

When we got to the hospital, I noted Christopher, the physician assistant from Pennsylvania (the PA from Pa.) who further advanced my new theory that, especially in Asheville, "Good-looking people go into medicine."

That young man put five stitches in Paul, to close up the worst of his cuts, chatting amiably all the while. He and his wife and four kids transplanted to Asheville a few years back (again—the trend of young families leaving populated urban areas for a more wholesome life in western North Carolina).

So, the splendid team of Asheville's Emergency Medical Squad (EMS)…the physician's assistant at the hospital…all confirm my new theory that apparently, the best-looking people flock to the health care field in Asheville.

Now, my question? Does my theory (about good-looking people going into the medical industry) extend to other cities and regions?

North Carolina Back Roads:
Norman Rockwell's America

Yeah, we're known to toss some bottled water and a snack of cut-up apple into a plastic baggie and off we go, in the SUV, traveling through the hills of western North Carolina. We're noticeable: We've got the emblem for our books, *Grandpa and the Truck*, emblazoned all over our car. We get honked by truckers, too, when they see the back window of our SUV emblazoned with "www.grandpaandthetruck.com: Tribute to America's Truckers! You copy?"

After a punishing winter, uncharacteristic for the South (folks suggest we didn't go far enough South for our winter home—and after all, we did choose the mountains), we're anxious for the first 70+ degree weather we've had in what seems like a century.

When we course these back roads, I know why many artists live here, because each turn of the road presents a vista of unbelievable beauty...rolling hills...wheat fronds swaying in the breeze...ramshackle fences...skeletal remains of old barns, close to collapse but still standing upright....a burned-out-but-still-standing 18-wheeler. All invite an artist's rendering.

I attempt artistry with my camera. When I see a particularly-compelling scene, I leap out of the car (barely remembering to put the vehicle in "park"), fumble with glasses, uncock the camera, free up the lens, and ramp up the viewer.

Thank God for digital cameras because I designate most shots unappealing…unacceptable…or just plain awful. Then, I delete them. Why? The wind's blowing (hair wisps cloud the lens)… sun's too bright (prevents proper viewing)…I've lost the shot (gotta move quickly, especially with light and cloud formations).

But I persevere and try mightily to hold steady through it all.

You see, photo-shooting's how I unwind. I gotta get away from that damned computer (a writer's bane) and just take in the natural splendor.

But I find back-handed humor, often, on these back roads.

I love it when we follow a road for about ten miles and then come to the sign "Dead End." That's when I release a stream of invective, saying: "*##@@@## They couldn't have told us that ahead of time!?"

Nope, I've begun to think North Carolinians do this in some skewed attempt to say "Gotcha!" "Let's give these Northerners (there are a lot of us here) something to bitch about."

The wondrous hillside shots are what lures me to these roads. For instance, on Bell Creek Rd., up the road from Mars Hill, sits a crazy red barn, decked out in Christmas gear, even in April. After all, why take down those decorations, if you only have to put them up the next year?

Another characteristic of these back regions? With their dilapidated barns, antique rusted trucks, and outhouses still standing, they've become a canvas of life in an earlier time.

Speaking of barns, it took me eight years to realize that these North Carolina structures were built with wide spaces in their slats to allow air to cure the tobacco leaves hanging from rafters. (I thought Southern farmers just didn't know how to build.)

Directly across from our complex, on Reems Creek Rd., in Weaverville, is the cutest little herd of mini-donkeys (I just love them!). They all saunter over to greet us and don't leave, either, when they figure out we've got no food. They just nudge their noses through the fence for a scratch, and I photo them, too.

So many regions of Asheville and surrounds offer a panoply of beauty that feeds my artist's soul.

Even a lowly outhouse sitting in a field is grist for the artist's palette.

Bonus Booklet: Realtor's Mini-Guide for Buying/Selling Property...Anywhere

Buying and Selling Property

In previous pages of this book, I've attempted to share with you (the reader), our experience in this wonderful land and offer you safeguards to help you in home purchase and sale–anywhere. I always felt: If I merely listed realtor tips, my message wouldn't carry as clearly, so I sought to share our personal story of buying and selling, with interesting details about our life in that region.

I will say: As a professional realtor, I was stunned at the number of folks who came into Asheville, from other parts of the country, drove around, and bought from the agent whose name they saw on a "For Sale" sign on property–a person who represented the seller.

Or, they bought the property from the agent they'd met at an Open House, a realtor who similarly represented the seller's interests.

Most never sought a realtor to act as their Buyer Broker, a professional who owes his or her fiduciary responsibility to the buyer.

When we knew we wanted to buy, in Asheville, we enlisted the help of a realtor. Since she worked for a large real estate company, it was no surprise that we ended up buying a townhome marketed by her company. I recognized she was a Seller Broker, but I didn't fear the situation, for I am schooled in real estate; I know to ask the right questions; and I doggedly get the answers.

But most folks don't have that training. They come in blind and buy blind.

In some cases, their purchase can be catastrophic, as one particular instance in a later chapter will demonstrate.

To that effect, I explain the different designations of realtor and how you might use their expertise optimally. I tell you, too, how you might self-sell.

I'll also tell you what situations may leave you at risk.

How Realtors Get Paid (and Why You Need to Understand This)

For the purposes of the next two chapters, I delineate most realtors as Buyer Broker, Seller Broker, or Transactional Realtor/Facilitator. I use the terms Broker and Realtor interchangeably, though they technically convey different meaning.

But there is another instance, too—that of Dual Agent, when the realtor owes limited fiduciary duties to both buyer and seller. (In some states, such a relationship is disallowed.)

Most people have no clue as to how a realtor is paid. Many think the realtor's company pays some type of salary to him or her, but that is almost never the case. A realtor is only paid when a property closes, the transaction whereby the realtor represents the buyer.. seller....or both.

As Buyer Broker, in Rhode Island, I helped people identify what they wanted in a home; and I protected their interests, writing up terms of the contract, overseeing inspections, suggesting areas of negotiation, bringing all to conclusion.

Most new realtors act in Buyer Broker mode, helping their clients find homes, for these realtors are building their client base. In fact, they may work for a buyer, with no recompense, if no sale takes place. That situation happened to me on more than one occasion.

When a home sale or purchase takes place, a Buyer Broker commission is generally paid from the Seller (Listing) Broker's commission, one usually split, in equal parts. For instance, if the seller agreed to a 6% commission to the real estate company he hired to sell his property, each realtor (one for buyer and one for seller) usually gets 3%.

Realtors never really get that full amount, for they must pay their brokerage firm a split, as well, so what looks like a windfall, initially, becomes less so by the end. As realtors succeed in business, their split with the company becomes more favorable to the realtor.

In some cases, however, realtors split the commission inequitably. Some Seller Brokers give their own selling company the lion's share of the commission, as in a 4%/2% scenario. The listing information on the Multiple Listing Service (MLS) only tells a Buyer Broker what his or her commission will be. It doesn't specify the full commission. The Buyer Broker will not realize the full commission until the closing when the amount due the selling company is clearly noted on the HUD (Housing and Urban Development) sheet where the breakdown of funds is shown.

A Buyer Broker should always have a client agree, in writing, regarding what that realtor's commission will be, for a Buyer Broker may expend significant time, gas, and energy and then, if pay is not determined, ahead of time, that realtor may forfeit pay, if the buyer moves forward in "For Sale By Owner" (FISBO in the trade.)

As a new realtor, I worked for weeks with an executive coming into Rhode Island, helping him identify his family's home. He told me he counted on me to sell his less-than-excited wife on the idea of a move from New Jersey to Rhode Island, making her aware of all the positives of our state.

When she arrived, I picked her up each day, from their rental apartment and drove her to yet another section of our state. I used my gas, put significant mileage on my car, and even bought her lunch on two occasions. The time I spent with her made me unavailable to work with others. But I failed to do what I should have done, at the outset–have her husband and her sign a Buyer Broker contract, specifying my commission.

In the end, I got nothing for my efforts because the husband determined to go forward on a For Sale By Owner (FIS-BO, in the trade.) He said he was "Sorry," but "I won't be using your professional help, after all." He offered me $1,000 (a third, of which I'd still give my company), which was insulting, considering how much time I'd spent. (Remember, in usual scenario, if $300,000 were selling price of home, 3% of the 6% selling commission–$9000– would go to buyer broker's company and my pay would have been approximately $5000.)

I declined his meager offer, but I was furious.

I told him it was my extensive help that allowed him to determine what they wanted in a property, by a process of elimination. In addition, I trained them in all aspects of home purchase, as we looked, and I'd been their tour guide, for weeks. But the lesson was one I never forgot.

A buyer's ultimate purchase is often just as much about what he doesn't want as what he does want, and he doesn't always know preferences up front.

In my Buyer Broker capacity, I helped other clients identify priorities, such as: "Is quick route to work a necessity?" "Is a town center important?" (because many towns don't have). "Are schools of prime importance?" "Is the municipal tax rate critical?" I helped them with radon and well water tests, notified them of dump site proximity and a host of more.

My buyers and I honed the search process, throughout. Sometimes this process took months. The quick identification of a property and entry into contract were the exceptions.

This recognition of how realtors are paid is important for all—especially for FSBO's to understand, for if a FSBO listing offers a lower than usual commission, when all other properties give buyer realtor 2.5% and 3%, that FSBO home will be at a serious market disadvantage.

In plain terms, let's say an average house price at $300,000, with 3% buyer broker commission results in $9000 to the realtor's company. The same house as FSBO, offering a 1.5 commission translates to a $4500 commission to the buyer broker company.

If you were the Buyer Broker (working weeks or months with a buyer/client), to whose home would you bring clients?

Disclaimer: Real Estate laws and principles are state-specific and are continually updated, so do check which are relevant to your situation. Since I am no longer a licensed professional realtor (I'm retired), I offer all information solely as "guide;" it's incumbent on the buyer/seller to perform his/her own "due diligence" (explained later.)

Is Your Realtor Really "Your Realtor"?

When we first came into Asheville on that Friday evening, a street fair was going on, and we heard rhythmic drum-beating in the distance. In other words, we were met with a festive scene which heralded good things for our first impression of this town set in the Blue Ridge Mountains.

On the crowded street was a temporary realtor booth set up, manned by a female realtor. I knew one thing—this realtor was relatively new to the region, for seasoned professionals do not generally seek clients in this manner. Rather, they rely on referrals from past customers.

I was correct. She'd lived in Asheville only a year. I took her business card, anyway.

Over the next several days, I interviewed a few realtors (with the idea one would become our Buyer Broker), but I kept going back to this one whom we'd met at the street fair, for I felt most comfortable with her. Yes, her being relatively new to the region was a negative, for I believed she couldn't know local issues that could affect us, but I was impressed with her manner, her professionalism, and her attention to detail.

But because we ultimately decided to buy a townhome that her company represented, as selling agent, she was never our Buyer Broker who owed her fiduciary duty to us.

Now, technically, a realtor acts in Buyer Broker mode if that is a designation a buyer insists on, and that buyer and realtor have signed a document attesting to her role as such.

Sometimes, a buyer in the course of a search will end up buying a property whose seller is represented by that same company for which the buyer's realtor works. (This happens often with bigger real estate companies that list many homes.) In that instance, and to avoid Dual Agency, the Broker/Owner of that company can assign an in-house realtor as Designated Seller Broker, representing the seller side, and the Buyer's Realtor can represent the buyer's interests.

As a realtor, myself, I wasn't bothered by the fact our realtor also represented the selling company, for I knew the important questions to ask. I wished to know: asking and selling price of all townhomes in the complex; how long they were on the market before they sold; if they were under contract with another buyer, any Back-on-Market homes (obviously, those sales fell through).

In other words, I wanted to know information professional realtors were privy to.

In many states (Florida is one), most realtors are moving away from the Buyer Broker designation (which portends a greater liability for realtor), acting instead as Transaction Realtors. In that instance, they owe limited representation to a buyer, a seller, or both, in a real estate transaction, but they do not represent either in a full fiduciary capacity. They merely facilitate the sale—a most important distinction a buyer or seller will want to consider.

There are only two capacities whereby realtors represent one party's interests, alone—that of Buyer Broker or Seller Broker.

But no matter where realtors work, they are expected to be honest and professional in their interaction with the public.

A buyer must recognize the role of his or her realtor and that person's fiduciary responsibility in order to make sound decisions. Ask for clarification if there is any doubt, and be mindful of the fact that these designations are puzzling to the best minds—even realtors'.

Why is this understanding important? I once knew a couple who sold their home in upstate New York, but the sale dragged on for almost a year from the signing of the purchase and sale to the closing, as time was extended, time and again, to the buyers in their efforts to get the best financing. All the while, the sellers paid huge mortgage payments, so the initial sale price resulted in far less to them, in the end. Why was this long, drawn-out process allowed (with contractual extensions given)? My suspicion is that the realtor acted in dual agent capacity and wanted to collect the full 6% commission, allegedly representing both buyer and seller. Obviously, one of those parties got the far better end of that transaction.

Dates on a contract usually run from six to eight weeks from start to finish and are set and adhered to so this kind of manipulation can't occur.

It's important for the buyer to recognize the various realtor designations and how each can impact him or her.

State You Claim as "Primary Residence" Matters

Friends asked why we didn't rent first, in our decision to try living in another state. Frankly, I didn't want to move twice—from Rhode Island to a rental and then again, into an owned unit, since we had already decided North Carolina would be our retirement state.

Furthermore, home ownership allows one to claim expenses on tax forms. Renting affords no such deductions.

Asheville had been the darling of retirement towns in recent years, and we expected that upward trend to continue. The only problem? Shortly after we bought, the housing market tanked and the country went into financial free-fall. Financial institutions had been doling out mortgage money to people who never should have had loans (they had poor credit histories); however, those financial institutions weren't concerned with applicants' creditworthiness. They only wanted the transaction fees. Home values were greatly inflated and the entire situation created a house of cards scenario, sending our nation to near-depression status.

And because financing is more difficult for those intent on buying condominiums and townhomes (plural ownership jacks up the risk to lenders), and since many owners are involved, (folks who die, lose jobs, etc.), condominium units are often harder to buy and sell...especially in a tough market.

For my purposes in this book, I use the terms condominium and townhome synonymously.

In most well-run townhome communities, there's a cap on how many rentals are allowed, too, so an owner can't merely say "Well, if things get bad, I can always rent out my unit." Then, too, some townhome communities enable the same pool of owners to rent out their units year after year, disallowing others whose financial situation might require they rent them out, if they can't sell.

However, that rent, for the owner, minus expenses, is taxable income.

During the years of the financial meltdown, many new condominium complexes in Asheville sat unoccupied, victims of a weak market. Years later, many of those complexes still hadn't recovered.

In buying into another geographic region, make sure you take into account all taxes. As stated earlier, in Weaverville, North Carolina, property owners pay both a town tax and a county tax and if you are a North Carolina resident, a state income tax (Rhode Island has all except the county tax.)

Maybe the region you consider has a high gasoline tax (a consumer product you use often). The sale tax on other items might be higher.

Some former Rhode Island residents suffered an unexpected new problem when they owned a home in Rhode Island and another in Florida which they newly claimed as primary residence. Yes, they avoided the Rhode Island state income tax, but in claiming Florida as primary residence, their Rhode Island home became eligible as second home, taxable as capital gain, when sold.

This new designation became especially significant if their home had risen in value from a hypothetical $200,000 to $450,000, over the years. The capital gain of $250,000 now more than equaled the savings realized when the former Rhode Island residents avoided the state income tax by claiming Florida (or other no-state-income-tax) home as primary residence.

It is ever important in decision-making, regarding finances, that one understands the consequences of actions and compares owning homes in different states in apples-to-apples manner.

How might a two-state home owner mitigate the problem, if one finds himself facing a tax consequence like this? Perhaps reclaim Rhode Island home (or whatever state where you have more exposure to capital gains tax) residence as primary residence for whatever the minimum is (three years?).

Now, the profit on the Rhode Island home, once sold, will not be taxed as capital gain.

That Annoying "Two-State Shuffle"

G oing back and forth between two states, every year, is problematic, but one only discovers this, in doing it.

The major deterrent is cost of maintaining both houses.

But there are other reasons you might not want to do the two-state shuffle:

Traveling the route twice a year—to and fro—gets really old fast. In the first years, it was OK but then I got to know the landscape and resented the traffic, the tie-ups, the waste of time, not to mention the need to stop over at least once, at a hotel, en route (fourteen hours is just too much to do in other-than-two, seven hour stretches.)

When you live elsewhere for a period of months, you invariably miss something you really need—such as a document for taxes, a receipt slip so you can return something, a favorite coat or jacket. They sound like high-class problems, but they amount to real annoyance over time.

You leave friends and lose your footing. In my case, I never could get rooted to a writing community because just as I was beginning to connect, I had to leave. Friends in either place regarded me as transitory, and they stopped investing heavily in our relationship (or at least, this was my experience).

You're not "real" to either group.

We put significant mileage on our car (we did fourteen hundred miles, just in getting to and fro) which affects its value, and when we were in North Carolina, all our car records were back in Rhode Island, so I wasn't sure what we'd had repaired (for instance, the expensive air filter and water pump might have been replaced, twice, in too short a time period).

When I still worked as a realtor (the first two years we were in Asheville), I lost a lot of money when I had to have other realtors in Rhode Island take over my listings when I was gone. I also felt guilty I was no longer the one representing my sellers, since they hired me—not my replacements.

Fortunately, no transaction suffered, but I worried that it would.

We couldn't take leadership positions, in either location, because we were literally "on the fly." In Rhode Island, I took on the role of Master of Ceremonies for a group called "Lively Literati," whereby I introduced our state's authors to audiences, but I had to get someone to cover for me five months of the year, when we went to North Carolina.

Then I had to reestablish myself in that role, when I came back to serve from May through December.

Paul couldn't be a member of the Board of our housing complex in North Carolina because we were part-time residents. (They wanted someone who lived there twelve months of the year.)

I lost significant opportunity to shop my books to the places most likely to support them (elementary schools in Rhode Island), for I basically had the limited period from October to December, during which I could do this. Fall was lost due to students acclimating to a new school year and multiple holidays in that stretch intervened, and when I returned to Rhode Island, in May, the end of the school year was approaching.

We bought duplicate items and household furnishings for the second home and then when we sold that home, we needed to sell or give away all—or suffer the inconvenience and finance of shipping them back to original house, from which we then sold them or gave them away.

How did all this shuffling affect me? I felt like a person without a country.

Now, I'm sure some people slide easily back and forth between locations, easily, but I must say: I found the simplest things problematic (How do I hook up my computer in my second location? That printer didn't talk to and align with my computer and I didn't remember how I connected them before.)

The best advice another two-state resident ever gave me: Print up a list of items to do before you close up that house for months and post the list so you can refer to it each time. This helps alleviate frustrations.

Yep...these are the unconsidered problems of the two-state resident.

Rent Storage Units?
Not This Boomer

My parents (and many of their generation) occupied the same home, practically all their lives. When it came time for them to leave that household, we "kids" pooled our energy to clear what amounted to 50+ years of living. We kept many of the inherited items, but only for a while, since we had more than enough of our own household possessions.

All across America, countless storage facilities dot the landscape. In the regions where seniors relocate (North/South Carolina, Florida, Georgia), those vast corrugated metal holding zones are everywhere–gated communities in their own right. Whole villages of them spring up—answering a crazy need for elders to hang on to their stuff.

Why are they so prevalent? Because older people, today, save furniture, household equipment, and personal artifacts, in the belief their adult "kids" will want them some day. And they're paying big for that service. That's why the storage business is booming.

But, here's the reality. Generally speaking, that furniture will never fit the lifestyle or décor of the intended recipients and unless the items are true antiques, their value is negligible (and storage costs will quickly eclipse that value).

So, it might be better for parents to offer the stuff they no longer want to the "kids" well before any intended move. That way, whatever isn't appropriated could go to the Salvation Army, Big Sisters, or consignment shops, to be used by someone who needs.

I know I've begun (over several years) to divest myself of stuff I collected over the years, and I've found it liberating. The house has a clean, uncluttered look, a blank palette, so to speak, on which I'll write my remaining years. Why do I especially like that look? I'm not tripping over memories of what used to be.

It's a good feeling, too, that whatever future moves we need effect won't require an army to accomplish...maybe just a few foot soldiers.

My new motto as a senior (younger people might also consider subscribing) is "Divest and simplify." I want to be able to pull up roots and move fast (even if I go nowhere). A wagonload—or 18-wheeler–of "stuff" will hamper me in those efforts.

I learned many years ago, when we made our last move, that most of the items we paid substantial money for–to be brought to the new house– were never used. They were stored in the attic, in the same boxes they arrived in. As a result, we paid all that money for nothing.

At the end of the day, who wants faded sheets and comforters in the new house...old pillows...records without an LP player (unless they're mint condition classics, in their own pristine jackets)?

What's the life trajectory for most older folks? Their route follows leaving a home or apartment...then going into a retirement home, followed by entry into an assisted living facility (perhaps all in the same building). Each move necessitates a winnowing of their possessions. I know—we went through this process with my mother. At her last move, into the nursing home, she ended up with a twin bed, bureau, and upholstered chair, along with a few framed photos. We needed to get rid of all else.

Young adults might consider "Divest and simplify," too.

Before marriage and children, they tend to move often, as jobs mandate or roommate situations present. The fewer encumbrances to a move, the better. They might consider inflatable furniture (retailers already offer this for beds and chairs) which will enable fluidity of movement, saving them substantial capital outlay.

And then there's the reality that young people haven't identified their personal style yet, and don't need to pay high cost for something they may devalue later. I remember liking the heavier Mediterranean-style furniture, as a young woman, and being happy, years later, that I hadn't bought a household of it (didn't have the money).

In the end, it may only be wise to accumulate things (sports equipment, household furnishings) when one begins raising a family and moves are no longer imminent. Wiser, still, are folks who recycle everything, for they never have a great deal to eliminate, thus saving themselves and the landfills.

So, this realtor's recommendation "Divest and simplify"… a motto that fits today's ever-more-transient population.

Hidden Monsters--Superfund Sites

"Caveat Emptor"--Let the Buyer Beware

Why should you care about Superfund sites? (Note—It's not "Superfun" sites.) Because you might become the inadvertent owner of property you thought wonderful, at first, only to discover its proximity to a toxic site listed by the government as one of the nation's worst offenders to public health.

As homeowner, you may expose your family to cancer-causing elements. Then, too, what happens when you try to sell? Savvy buyers who research their intended purchase will find the information you didn't, and they'll steer clear of purchase.

As for remediation of toxins at that site? No one is sure how, when, or even "if" that will happen.

Unfortunate and uninformed purchase could have happened to us. After all, as buyers, we were coming into a region we knew little about, and as we all have learned in life, things are almost never as they appear.

Paul's naïve in the way he trusts that things are what they seem. For instance, on a restaurant menu, in Burnsville, western North Carolina, he saw trout featured and asked "Is the fish from a local stream?" In his mind's eye, he envisioned a fly fisherman enticing the fish from a clear mountain stream, the purity of both, assured.

What do I see, in mine? Hidden danger...pollution...toxic chemicals in that stream.

The waitress answered: "No, you wouldn't want that. Our fish is farm trout" (meaning it's raised in a supervised facility).

Her message is clear: One can't always tell how pure something is by how it looks.

Because I was raised in a mill town, where I'd learn the beautiful, purple-blue waters were chemical dyes in streams, and due to the knowledge I gained in my second career as professional realtor, I know to be concerned about issues affecting home ownership, particularly factors that are subterranean and out of view.

With that in mind, I was especially cautious about out-of-state purchase of property, and I expressed my concerns to our North Carolina realtor: "I want no home near a Superfund site."

I didn't merely leave the investigating to her, either. At night, on my computer, I checked the government's listing of forty-two Superfund sites, in North Carolina, to insure none of the proposed properties we visited were near one.

I'd learn about other western North Carolina buyers who weren't so fortunate.

Today, on a back road, heading out of Hendersonville, south of Asheville, in a seemingly idyllic part of town, is the upscale community of Southside Village whose original residents were unaware of any future negative impact regarding their home purchase.

Next to that gated community, behind a locked chain link fence, signs warn folks to "Keep Out!" Behind that fence are the leveled remains of a factory whose chunks of concrete and asphalt are sole physical remnants of a plant once dedicated to metal plating and electronic production. This factory, the former CTS plant, operated from 1959 to 1986, producing electronic components of tin, nickel, zinc, and silver, used in automobile parts and hearing aids.

Workers cleaned components with TCE (trichloroethylene), and according to ATSDR (the Agency for Toxic Substances and Disease Registry), "TCE is a nonflammable, colorless liquid with a somewhat sweet odor and a sweet, burning taste, used mainly as a solvent to remove grease from metal parts, but it is also an ingredient in adhesives, paint removers, typewriter correction fluids, and spot removers."

At the time of the plant's operation, workers disposed of the TCE by pouring it down cement drains leading out onto the property or letting it leach down through the ground.

The immediate site of the plant was ten acres with another forty-four acres surrounding it.

In 1997, the Mills Gap Road Association (owners of the land of the former CTS plant) sold part of that acreage to the Biltmore Group and in 1998, that group began building Southside Village. As to how such a building permit was given, considering what some knew of nearby contaminants, that appears a mystery.

At present, there is no definitive proof that the gated community of Southside Village is affected, regarding the quality of its soil or air (these are continually monitored), for as some have stated: Lots on which the houses sit are higher up and groundwater doesn't travel uphill. Then, too, Southside Village's homes are connected to city water.

Others are not so fortunate. Beneath the concrete slab of the CTS building site, a plume of chemical contaminants moves silently, potentially posing risk of air and water pollution to nearby residents—especially those who rely on well water.

The Rice family whose property abuts the former CTS site demonstrates why it's critical to know what has transpired on or near property one considers for purchase. Terry Rice is the current owner, inheriting the property from his grandfather who bought the land in 1974. On it, the older Rice built a cabin, the home Terry Rice currently occupies.

As a boy, Terry drank water from that stream and swam in it. The family used that water for its household needs. He now believes the many cancers affecting his family are a direct result of contamination of water (and air) from proximity to that CTS plant.

According to government records, the Environmental Protection Agency (EPA) knew, as early as 1991, that there were toxins in the mountain stream on the Rice property but nobody told the family (The *Atlantic*, March 5, 2015). It was only when a friend of Terry's noted dead plants at the edge of the water and a strange diesel odor, that he suggested testing that water. Results showed a significant level of TCE, 4,200 times the state environmental standards, was present.

As of 2012, the former CTS site is now listed as "Active," on the National Priorities List Superfund site, designated so by the Environmental Protection Agency, in response to CERCLA (the Comprehensive Environmental Response, Compensation, and Liability Act, commonly known as Superfund).

This law created a tax on the chemical and petroleum industries and provided broad Federal authority to respond directly to releases or threatened releases of hazardous substances that may endanger public health or the environment.

The national government website listing Superfund sites in any state is epa.gov/Superfund/search-Superfund-sites-where-you-live. Three Superfund sites are listed in Buncombe County, the region we identified for our future home: CTS, at 295 Mills Gap Rd., Asheville; Chemtronics, at 180 Old Bee Tree Rd., in Swannanoa; and the site of Blue Ridge Plating, Glenn Bridge Rd., in Arden. They appear as "active" on the National Priorities List (NPL).

Of the forty-seven thousand waste sites, nationwide, seventeen hundred have been declared Superfund sites. North Carolina has forty- two.

In this book, I do not reference any North Carolina Non-National Priorities List sites (not considered as posing serious threat), nor do I list any that have been remediated. I also have not referenced any of the hundreds of military bases currently flagged by the EPA (Erin Brockovich's new cause for how it has affected the health and well-being of military people and their families) for ground water contamination, but you may wish to check out proximity of your intended purchase to one of these (especially if said purchase depends on well water).

What would I say to future property owners concerned about environmental issues and how they might impact property purchase? Search Superfund and toxic waste sites in multiple ways. In other words, be proactive. As to sites that may not be listed but could still pose potential harm, this realtor recommends potential property buyers ride around the region and note signs of past industry. Ask senior staff at Town or City Halls and residents if there have been any factories in the region, in the past. Find out what they produced. If remains or ruins of old factories exist on site, Google search the address, to discover what factory operated there, originally.

The good news today? Buyers can find out such information. In an earlier era, this information was unavailable or buyers were at the mercy of unscrupulous realtors or builders who cared little about a buyer's stated concerns.

As buyer or seller, it's important to do your own research—and not rely on others.

In November 2016, a story in the *Asheville Citizen Times* focused on recent decision-making regarding the CTS clean-up. It's important to note, however, that continued commitment to clean-up is dependent upon federal funds allocated for that agency and those in administrative capacity. As of this publication, there's been a significant reduction in funding to EPA (one third slash under the Trump administration), and a new head of the Environmental Protection Agency, Scott Pruitt, has taken over, one whom many fear is less committed to that agency's original purpose.

The above sign designates the CTS Superfund site, next to Southside Village. How a track of land appears at ground level may belie what's happening underground.

On another note, residents of Rhode Island (or any state) might find information on Superfund sites in their region equally compelling. At present, there are twelve Superfund sites listed for Rhode Island. (We hosted a bustling jewelry industry and the Quonset Point Naval Station.)

Little Rhody is home to two hundred toxic sites.

It's not just Superfund and toxic dump sites that can adversely affect value, either. I once knew a realtor whose daughter bought a condominium above what appeared to be a sweet neighborhood coffee shop in Boston. The buyer had only checked out her intended purchase during the day. At night, the little coffee shop had a whole new character, morphing into a club scene with liquor license. This buyer was quite upset with the noise that ruled from 9:00 P.M. on...But she was stuck.

A buyer must always employ "due diligence" (a phrase in real estate, meaning "do your homework"..."find out the facts"..."be informed") or pay the price.

Sometimes, that price may be one's life savings and much more.

Successful Home Buyer's Checklist

Remember: The realtor only gets paid if the house sale takes place (the closing). And most often, the buyer realtor commission comes out of the seller's proceeds (usually half of the listing real estate company's commission.) The only time commission may not be clear is in instances when buyer moves forward on a For Sale By Owner (which is why the Buyer Broker commission should be determined ahead of time, and in writing). What do I suggest if, as Buyer, you are hesitant about signing a contract because you don't know the realtor? Go out on a couple of home tours; determine the fit; then sign, if comfortable. This is a protection for you both.

1. Research and determine the best places to invest in today's real estate market; there are regions of the country experiencing growth and acceleration of value, while other markets demonstrate flat or negative return on value.

2. Make a Wish List of important attributes you want in a property. Just as important, list what you do *not* want. Communicate both to your realtor; you cannot blame your realtor if you do not make clear your preferences (i.e. "Nothing near a Superfund Site, landfill, or waste water treatment facility" are examples of concerns).

3. Interview potential Buyer Brokers to advocate for your interests (this even applies to buyers purchasing new construction through a builder). Go on tour with realtor to determine the fit. A realtor in your home state can set you up with one in your destination state (they usually get a referral fee). State in writing how the commission will be paid (especially in purchase of For Sale by Owner home). Some realtors are "transactional realtors," owing no specific allegiance to any one party but are there to see the sale goes through. Know the difference.

4. Beware Dual Agency (it's disallowed in some state) when the realtor represents you, the buyer, and the company marketing the property (seller). This relationship is the least protective of the buyer and if you persist in purchase, you will need to be your own advocate. Ask to see *all* recent comparable property data, called "the comps." (solds, pendings and "for sales" both in complex (if condominium) and those in neighboring towns. Determine the history of the unit or home you consider (Was it ever on the market in the past? How long was it offered? What was asking and sale price?) With that information, you can assess all, determine fair market value, and negotiate wisely.

5. Remember that sale price is only one aspect. If you can be flexible on closing date and other issues, you might negotiate price or garner upgrades, especially if you do not HAVE to sell one property as a contingency to purchase another.

6. Enumerate items on Purchase & Sale (contract) that you expect to convey:

   For instance, *specify* refrigerator, stove, and dishwasher, as opposed to just including "appliances." In some states, "appliances" is arbitrary. Just as important, include what will be removed, if resale: "Underground oil tank will be removed" or "unused oil tank in basement will be removed prior to closing." Clarifying items in writing makes misunderstanding less likely.

7. Have professional, licensed person inspect the property (if new construction, this can occur at Walk-thru). Develop Punch List (if new construction)—the list of things needing remedy. If older property, inspection is usually held within specified time following contract (often two weeks). Buyer Broker will communicate requests to the other side, in writing, agreement is mutual as to remedy or credit, in writing.

8. Authorize a radon test and request mitigation system or credit for same if radon is higher than 4.0, *if that is agreeable to you.* If home has well water, test water for radon as well as for quality (a system to purge radon in water and air is extremely costly). If these levels are unacceptable to you, request release from contract, in writing, in the specified allowed time. The time for all inspections and information gathering is set forth in the contract (that timeframe is called Due Diligence in North Carolina). Buyers and sellers must adhere to dates or forfeit rights.

9. Withhold funds (escrow) from seller at closing, if something is not done per contract (i.e. house of former owner not cleaned out, at closing...oil tank not removed).

10. Read and understand community restrictions (condo documents or by-laws) to make certain you can live with those (some outlaw RV's, pets, a satellite dish, etc.). You will be signing off on this but give those condo documents a serious read ahead of time.

11. Hire moving company, if applicable, and establish dates for utilities (gas, electricity, water.)

12. Ask to see HUD sheet *before closing* (this is the form that lists all costs and any payouts for buyer and seller). In this way, there will be no surprises at closing. If there is a figure you do not understand, ask the closing attorney to explain.

13. Write down building contractor (or foreman's) cell number for questions on new construction that will arise, post-closing, and get list of all utility contractors you might need (plumbing, electrical, etc.).

14. Print copy of this and post in place where you can refer to it, often.

15. Join committees, if you buy into a condominium community, to insure you are aware of issues; this will further facilitate adjustment. It's much easier to be on the ground floor of decision-making, as opposed to trying to change rules later.

16. Be patient. It takes time to remedy issues, find new friends, discover the best places to get what you need, etc. You are beginning a whole new life in a new land.

17. Enjoy the journey.

Successful Home Seller's Checklist

Before selling, get Comparative Market Analyses (CMA's) from three professional realtors from different companies in the region who will provide information on all comparable properties regarding asking price/selling price of properties similar to yours. These CMA's are done free of charge, since realtors hope that you will choose one of them to represent you in the event your property doesn't sell via your efforts. The following will facilitate a sale.

1. Paint walls neutral (like Pottery Barn bisque) or some similar hue on walls (I've seen visceral reactions in some buyers when they first note blue, green, or coral walls.) Remove wall art (if dramatic) with care and fill holes with paint tinted to match (Ace Hardware matches paint, as well as Home Depot). Paint entire walls when necessary.

2. Provide a clean, uncluttered horizon. Store away multiple appliances from countertops, remove knickknacks, and all personal artifacts from the visual field, to enable the prospective buyer to "see" the room.

3. Remove any holiday decorations, if they are still up during non-holiday times.

4. Remove fixtures that will not pass with the property, ahead of time (family heirloom chandelier hanging over dining room table).

5. Highlight areas that are especially positive (you might note "engineered" hardwoods, as opposed to laminates.) Note the separate heating/cooling control for the second floor and door/wall differentiating it from the loft effect of similar models. If a realtor represents your home, make sure he/she knows these facts. Write all the extras on a sheet so realtor can highlight for potential buyers. Post in highly accessible spot for showings.

6. If you self-sell, add your home to a list-only service to get your property into a multiple listing so realtors see it.

7. Place your property and many photos on Zillow. Include important shots of washer and dryer, furnace and plumbing, oversized, uncluttered garage, attractive grounds. On that listing, you state the buyer broker commission, if that is your intention (examples are 2.5%, if 5% is the usual listing rate in your region, or 3% if 6% is the norm.) According to Zillow, the best day of the week to list your property is Thursday, and the best month is May (although those times will vary by the market). Check with that site for information on your region.

8. Fill out the disclosure forms, accurately, and seek on-line information, if you do not understand some terms. (For Sale By Owner kits are available at retail outlets like Staples, Walmart, Home Depot.)

9. If you do hire a real estate agency, make sure you exclude names of potential buyers (only one or two) who were interested in the property during the period you attempted

to sell. (Give them limited time period, for they may still come forward.) If they do, you may still commission a realtor to represent you in inspections, negotiations, etc., on a sliding fee basis, of course. Negotiate.

10. Determine commission. There is no set, firm commission for selling. Some agencies want 6%...Others 5%. Ask how they will split with a buyer broker. (You want "equitable" to entice Buyer Brokers.) A low buyer broker commission will discourage Buyer Brokers who have been working with some buyers for significant time, in some cases.

11. Adhere strictly to all dates set forth in the contract.

12. If you go the self-sell route and your buyer is a "cash buyer," get a pre-approval letter stating that the buyer has the funds from a recognized bank or financial institution. (It's often considered riskier to have a cash buyer in that money can be spent anytime, whereas financing is a several weeks' investment of buyer's time and effort.)

13. If self-sell, direct lawyer to make up the contract based on seller's and buyer's agreed-upon terms. These are standard forms used in the state where the principals reside.

14. As seller, you'll probably want your own lawyer. Ask ahead of time what duties they perform, as your representative. For instance, "When do you (or your representative) turn over the keys?" (The closing doesn't assure the property sale is registered, and until that time, you're still officially the owner and liable.) "Will lawyer make sure the sale is registered at Town or City Hall?" "Will they check that you got your money—if it was supposed to be wired into your account?"

15. If you go the self-sell route, and you've been interacting with the proposed buyer, and then at some future time

that buyer brings in a Buyer Broker, realize that you (as seller) are not obliged to honor that Buyer Broker commission for that realtor was not the "procuring cause" (an uninterrupted series of causal events that led to the purchase of the property).

16. Recognize that the usual window of time for home purchase/sale contract may be six to eight weeks, during which principals can plan for household packing and delivery and all aspects of contract met (inspections, negotiations, financial obligations, etc.). We self-packed as well, meaning we bought boxes from a packing company and packed daily so we wouldn't face a mountain of work at the last minute. Early in the process, we hired our moving person, after checking on his references.

17. Contact utility companies (electric, gas, cable, water) with date for shut-off, at a time after date of closing (to allow for any unforeseen delays).

18. Notify post office of change in seller's address.

19. Determine tax cost from municipal authority (we had both Weaverville and Buncombe County taxes).

20. Print out and keep a copy of this seller's checklist.

21. Consider all of the above "one day at a time"—not the mountain of details it first appears. Check off the check-off list as you perform the actions.

***My suggestions in this book are meant as a guide and are by no means to be considered set in stone. This is the process we used in our successful sale, while I note aspects that became a problem (i.e. arrival of a supposed buyer broker...the lawyers, etc.).

Acknowledgments

I would like to thank the following for their help in the production of this book:

Jacqueline Damian of Pennsylvania who graciously slogged through and edited the earliest copy of *Boomerrrang*, providing me with invaluable input. If there are any other mistakes (and I'm sure there are), they are solely mine.

Carol Young, former Deputy Executive Editor of the Providence Journal, whose edits for another book of mine became an unexpected part of this one.

Web designer **Steven Ruggieri** whose deft recrafting of my website (colleenkellymellor.com), book jacket design, and stellar marketing ideas have given me a presence on the worldwide web, enabling folks to find this book.

The folks who took time from their busy lives, to read and review my book: **David Iannuccilli, Ed Iannuccilli**, and **Gary Gallucci** (if they're all Italian, it's no accident; Rhode Island IS Italian).

The **people of Hamburg Crossing**, a most unique and supportive townhome community in Weaverville, Western North Carolina.

My **Asheville women's group** and another support group that will remain anonymous (you know who you are). Your help during our medical crisis was invaluable and I share your suggestions so others might be similarly successful.

My longtime partner, Paul Wesley Gates, a zany Arkansan by birth, Rhode Islander by choice, whose crazy antics over 25 years provide much fodder for my story-telling.

The **countless Rhode Island folks** who encouraged and supported my literary efforts over the years, allowing me to believe a Rhode Island milltown girl could actually rise to the lofty heights of "successful writer."

Ashevillians/Weavervillians/Western North Carolinians. You held us for almost ten years; in the end, you lost out to that quirky, littlest of states, Rhode Island, a giant for its diversity, great food, gorgeous natural scenery, and its major calling card–the ocean.

The Takeaway

*B*oomerrrang begins with a crash.
Then there's an explosion.

After Paul's horrific accident, his broken neck, his "death" due to choking, post-surgery, his ending up in ICU, and his frightening cognitive changes, I had simply endured all I was going to take from his arrogant neurosurgeon. My women friends (some with Southern accents) cautioned me: "Shhhhh.... Be nahce, Colleen (remember, they're Southern). You'll get far mo-ah with honey than you will with vin-a-gah."

Well, people had been telling me that my whole life, and frankly, I never found that to be the case. No, my experience has been that women get pushed around if they don't stand tall and insist on certain things.

So I took my almost 5'9" frame and did just that, and I'm sure that hospital neurosurgeon will never forget my heated delivery that day in that hospital room. Nor will the nurse witness. But I did get the results I hoped for.

That accidental lesson (to speak up against authority) might be one of *Boomerrrang*'s best, hidden values.

You see, most of *Boomerrrang,* is an invaluable guide for those buying and selling real estate. Especially those going out of state... and most especially, those going South.

But its many tips can be applied to property purchase/sale anywhere.

In this book, I share my knowledge as highly successful realtor and warn of the pitfalls for the uninformed. But I share that knowledge in a fun and humorous manner, by painting vignettes of our search for the perfect retirement home and our years, living in one of America's top retirement towns—Asheville, North Carolina.

A famous advertising campaign in the 70's warned us all to get an American Express credit card and "Don't leave home without it." That phrase applies to this book. If you're gonna buy property (anywhere), strap Boomerrrang to your hip and use it as a reference.

Or give it to a friend who will benefit from its tips.

Boomerrrang will discuss our search, the value of using a realtor's professional help, how we chose the state...town...the model we ultimately selected, the pros and cons of townhome/condo ownership, over single standing homes.

I tell how we ultimately sold our retirement home, ourselves, saving thousands, a prescriptive any seller might follow– no matter where he or she lives (even in Rhode Island).

As Boomers enter their retirement years and become the largest mobile population the United States has ever experienced, tens of thousands will head off into new territories for their later years.

Many will be oblivious as to how much risk they take on, by buying real estate, unaware.

Boomerrrang will help people avoid exposure to higher risk.

Our chosen town, Asheville, will remain a welcoming beacon for many who don't wish the homogeneity and frenetic pace of Florida or other deep southern enclaves.

It will remain a quirky town that keeps its rustic edge due its proximity to the glorious Blue Ridge/Smoky Mountains.

In other words, Asheville will ever fly under the banner of individualism.

Most of our years, there, were filled with enrichment and wonder. As such, we recommend Asheville for its diverse character, its artistic community; its commitment to preserving the earth (it's a green region); its wondrous food; its skilled and handsome medical personnel (even if they're too few); its gorgeous natural beauty that finally allowed me to know the meaning of 'purple mountains majesty' from "America the Beautiful."

Some say: "You don't choose the mountains; the mountains choose you."

If that is true, Paul and I are eternally grateful for being two of the chosen ones.

Made in the USA
Columbia, SC
25 February 2018